纪念白求恩

—格雷文赫斯特抒怀—

In Memory of Dr. Norman Bethune
—A Pilgrim Tribute to Gravenhurst of Canada (Expressivo)

忽培元 著

任小玫 译

熊　蕾 英文审定

Written by Hu Peiyuan

Translated by Ren Xiaomei

Revised by Xiong Lei

北京燕山出版社

BEIJING YANSHAN PRESS

图书在版编目（CIP）数据

纪念白求恩：汉、英 / 忽培元著；任小玫译. — 北京：北京燕山
出版社，2024.9

ISBN 978-7-5402-7283-8

Ⅰ.①纪… Ⅱ.①忽… ②任… Ⅲ.①诗集－中国－当代－汉、
英 Ⅳ.① I227

中国国家版本馆 CIP 数据核字（2024）第 110196 号

纪念白求恩：汉、英

著　　者：忽培元

译　　者：任小玫

执行编辑：殷　芳

责任编辑：满　懿

出版统筹：李　娜

封面绘画：忽培元

装帧设计：许　振

出版发行：北京燕山出版社有限公司

社　　址：北京市西城区琉璃厂西街 20 号

邮　　编：100052

电话传真：86-10-65240430（总编室）

印　　刷：天津市天玺印务有限公司

成品尺寸：145mm×210mm　1 / 32

字　　数：154 千字

印　　张：9.875

版　　次：2024 年 9 月第 1 版

印　　次：2024 年 9 月第 1 次印刷

书　　号：ISBN 978-7-5402-7283-8

定　　价：66.00 元

作者 2007 年 9 月在白求恩的故乡访问。

用生命的交响铸就高尚

"你以生命的交响，回答着什么是高尚。"

这是忽培元先生的长诗《纪念白求恩：格雷文赫斯特抒怀》中的一句，如全诗 22 个篇章中的每个诗句，炽热，深情，感人肺腑。

白求恩的一生，的确体现了用生命的交响铸就的高尚。

忽先生的诗句，把我带到枫叶之国白求恩的故乡格雷文赫斯特，让我回想起 2019 年 10 月下旬，我随同中国白求恩精神研究会的专家们，参加"纪念白求恩逝世 80 周年国际研讨会"的那些情景。那是我第一次有幸来到白求恩诞生的地方，也是第一次亲身经历东西方白求恩研究不同观点的碰撞。我从而对这位伟大的国际共产主义战士有了更深的了解，也与忽先生的长诗产生了共鸣。

纪念白求恩

诚如诗人的叙述，白求恩原本是"一个平凡而伟大的生命"，是"当过轮船侍者、伐木工、新闻记者、小学教员和医学学士的上尉医生"。他与中国共产党和中国人民相交于抗击法西斯的战火中，最后长眠在中国河北唐县的一个山村的农家院里。

在他去世 40 天之后的 1939 年 12 月 21 日，毛泽东主席在延安写下了《纪念白求恩》一文，高度赞颂白求恩是"一个高尚的人，一个纯粹的人，一个有道德的人，一个脱离了低级趣味的人，一个有益于人民的人"，号召"每个共产党员都要学习他"。从此，白求恩精神融入中国革命传统和主流价值观。看看在加拿大，研究、弘扬白求恩的基本上只限于个别有良知的学者，而在中国，白求恩精神研究会的领导者都是人民解放军的将军和高级军官，更有像忽先生这样的政府高级官员倡导学习白求恩，这是何等的反差！

在很长的时间里，白求恩在他的故国几乎默

默无闻。他在中国的热和在自己故乡的冷，也是一个巨大的反差。一位旅居加拿大多年的朋友告诉我，1970 年中加建交后，中国驻加拿大大使馆赠送了一个白求恩雕像给他曾经工作过 8 年的麦吉尔大学，居然遭到拒绝。原因是，他们不能接受一尊共产党人的雕像。后来几经周折，雕像才立在了大学所在的蒙特利尔市的一个街角。

就连格雷文赫斯特小镇的白求恩故居，也是因为众多中国"朝圣者"的驱动，才建成了纪念馆的。那也是在 20 世纪 70 年代中加建交后，来加拿大访问的中国团体几乎无一例外地前来造访，加拿大政府才出资买下了白求恩家的那所房子，建立起白求恩纪念馆。我听加拿大学者说，当年的加拿大总理老特鲁多，也就是现任加拿大总理的父亲，要加拿大外交部出钱买下白求恩故居时，还很受到一番非议，认为这是"讨好中国人"的举动，"没有必要"。

纪念白求恩

　　另一个巨大的反差，就是白求恩的形象在中国和加拿大及西方世界的截然不同，以及对他的解读。白求恩这个名字在中国家喻户晓，几乎是高尚的同义语。而西方主流舆论场中的白求恩，似乎就是"花花公子"、"风流情种"、脾气粗暴、放荡不羁。即使白求恩在 1936 年冬到 1937 年 6 月志愿去西班牙参加了反法西斯的内战，也做出了不凡的成绩，但是他依然没有被家乡人乃至同志视为英雄，反而是跟同一战壕的战友闹矛盾到了不可开交的地步而被遣返回加拿大。

　　然而，就如谚语所说，"鹰有时比鸡飞得还低，但鸡永远也飞不了鹰那么高"。即使加拿大舆论把白求恩贬得极低的时候，他们也不能否认白求恩医术的高超。而一句"对技术精益求精"，毛主席更是说透了白求恩的专业精神。那一句"白求恩同志毫不利己专门利人的精神，表现在他对工作的极端的负责任，对同志对人民的极端的热忱"中的两个

"极端"，又说透了白求恩的为人。毛主席可以称得上是白求恩真正的知音！

在 2019 年的研讨会上，我和与会者分享了我的一个亲身经历，来说明中国草根对白求恩的解读。那是 2008 年清明之前，我跟着一位网名"老普"的北京退休干部张保田，去河北易县一个名叫甘河净的山村。甘河净是抗战时期晋察冀边区八路军医院的一个医疗站，1939 年 10 月底的黄土岭战役中，白求恩在涞源孙家庄小庙抢救伤员时不慎割伤手指后，就是到甘河净对集中在那里的伤员做进一步治疗的。就是在甘河净，他在救治伤员时伤口再度感染。此时白求恩的身体已经非常虚弱，随行人员带着他往唐县的后方医院赶。然而到了一个叫石家庄子的村子，白求恩听说又一场战斗打响了，便不顾随行人员的劝阻，当即折返向北，想再度赶往前线。走到了旺家台，白求恩高烧不退，身体极度虚弱，却仍然要求凡是胸部和头部负伤的战士都必须送他检查。最后聂荣臻司令员下了死命令，白求恩才同意后撤。可是，到了距后方医院只有 6 公里的唐县黄石口村，白求恩已经病危，只好在那里住下。两天后，白求恩与世长辞。

"老普"画了一幅简图说明白求恩在生命的最后 10 天所走的路线。这条线从起点甘河净到终点黄石口，不是一条直线，而是一个大大的"之"字，就是因为他在生命垂危的时候，还要赶往前线，一直心系伤员。"老普"说，这个巨大的"之"字，就是白求恩生命的最后旅途，非常震撼人心。就从这一幅路线图，白求恩一心救治八路军伤员的奋不顾身，一目了然。这正是用生命的交响，铸就的高尚的最强音。

几十年过去，白求恩的伟大终于在他的故乡得到了承认。但是很多人对他的伟大追根溯源，追到了"基督精神"上，认为他的伟大源于他自幼受到的基督精神的熏陶。确实，往上数三代，白求恩的父亲、爷爷都是牧师。

不能否认家庭的传统宗教信仰对白求恩可能的影响。可是直到 20 世纪 30 年代中期白求恩去西班牙、去中国参加反法西斯战争，那时的人们除了认同他医术高超，可并不认为他是伟人。如果说白求恩的伟大源自基督精神的熏陶，那说他是"花花公子"、"风流情种"的时候，基督精神怎么就不见了踪影呢？

加拿大研究白求恩的权威历史学者拉瑞·汉纳特先生有一句评论给我印象很深。他说，一般人都是年轻的时候激进，随着年龄的增长思想越来越趋于平和。而白求恩却是年纪越大，思想越激进。他转向信仰共产主义是在 1935 年，他 45 岁的时候。那一年，白求恩加入了加拿大共产党。

应该说，白求恩自幼就有追求，从来就不平庸。这是造就他伟大的基础。他在去西班牙前给自己做了一个墓志铭："生为资产阶级，死为共产党人。"

那真是非同凡响。白求恩在西班牙也轰轰烈烈了一番，但是其影响远远不及他的中国之行。

为什么同一个白求恩在西班牙铩羽而归，却在中国走向了辉煌？我认为，就是因为白求恩遇到了中国共产党及其领导的八路军。中国共产党及其领导的八路军虽然老土，但是胸襟博大。这个党和这支人民军队的上上下下尊重他，却不是求着他、照顾他、惯着他，能够充分发挥他的才干却又能用纪律约束他。而这个党和军队的宗旨方略及行为方式，也让白求恩心悦诚服。所以他在这片土地上活得清贫而快乐。让他在西班牙和党内同志闹到不可开交的臭脾气，在中国就没有产生任何不愉快的后果。白求恩的臭脾气还在，他却和中国同志相处得很好，就是因为土八路"镇得住"他。所以，最终成就白求恩的伟大的，是中国共产党和八路军，白求恩在中国最终升华为高尚纯粹的人，成为我党我军光荣传统的一部分。

当然，我们不忘白求恩的共产主义信仰，并不是一定要不分时间地点对象地把意识形态挂在口头上。我们现在讲建设人类命运共同体，其实，白求恩就是践行建设人类命运共同体的先驱。所以，他的伟大，才能跨越时代，为所有善良的人所接受，所赞颂，他用生命的交响铸就的高尚，才能永远在我们心中回荡。

熊 蕾

2022 年 6 月 18 日

于北京木樨地

纪念白求恩

Nobility Forged by the Symphony of Life

"By the symphony of life

You show 'What is nobility?' in response. "

This is a line in Mr. Hu Peiyuan's long poem *In Memory of Dr. Norman Bethune: A Pilgrim Tribute to Gravenhurst of Canada (Expressio)*. Like every line in the 22 cantos of the poem, it is passionate, full of deep feeling, and touching.

Indeed, Bethune's life embodies the nobility forged by the symphony of life.

Mr. Hu's poem takes me back to Gravenhurst, the hometown of Dr. Bethune in the country of maple leaves, and reminds me of the scenes in late October 2019 when I participated in the "International Symposium to Commemorate the 80th Anniversary of Dr. Bethune's Death" with the experts of the Chinese Bethune Spirit

Research Association. It was the first time I had the privilege to visit the famous doctor's birthplace, and the first time I experienced a rendezvous of different perspectives on Bethune research in the East and the West. I thus gained a deeper understanding of this great international communist fighter and resonate with Mr. Hu's long poem.

As the poet recounts, Dr. Bethune was "a man, humble and great in infinity like a mote," who worked as "a civilian ship-waiter, a lumberjack, a journalist, a primary school teacher, also as a military captain with a medical bachelor's degree." He befriended the Communist Party of China and the Chinese people in the anti-Fascist war, and finally rested forever in a mountain village in Tangxian County of China's Hebei Province.

On December 21, 1939, 40 days after his death, Chairman Mao Zedong wrote an article in Yan'an entitled "In Memory of Norman Bethune", highly praising Bethune as "noble-minded and pure, a man of moral integrity and above vulgar interests, a man who is of value to the people, " and emphasizing that "every Communist must learn from him. " Since then, the spirit of Bethune has been fused into the Chinese revolutionary tradition and mainstream values. Look at the facts that in Canada, where the study and promotion of Bethune is basically confined to a few scholars with conscience, while in China, the leaders of the Bethune Spirit Research Association are generals and senior officers of the People's Liberation Army, and there are senior government officials like Mr. Hu who advocate learning from Bethune. What a striking contrast!

For a long time, Dr. Bethune remained almost unknown in his homeland. Adoration for him in China and indifference to him in his homeland are also a striking contrast. A Chinese friend who has lived in Canada for many years told me that after the establishment of diplomatic relations between China and Canada in 1970, the Chinese Embassy in Canada presented a statue of Bethune to McGill University, where Dr. Bethune had worked for 8 years, but was rejected, because the Canadian university could not accept a statue of a Communist. After several twists and turns, the statue was finally placed on a street corner in the city of Montreal, where the university is located.

Even the Bethune Memorial House in his hometown Gravenhurst was not built until after tides of Chinese "pilgrims" drove the local authorities to make it. It also happened after the establishment of diplomatic relations between China and Canada in the 1970s, when visiting Chinese delegations to Canada almost without exception paid pilgrimage to the small town, compelling the Canadian government to purchase the house of the Bethune family and turn it into the Bethune Memorial. I learned from Canadian scholars that when Canadian Prime Minister Pierre Elliot Trudeau, the father of the current Canadian prime minister, asked the Canadian Department of External Affairs to pay for the purchase, he was extensively criticized, arguing that this was a move to "please Chinese" and

纪念白求恩

"unnecessary."

Another striking contrast is the very different image of Bethune in China from that in Canada and the whole Western world, and the different interpretations of him. The name Dr. Bethune is well known in China and is almost a synonym of nobility. But the dominant image of Norman Bethune in the mainstream public opinion in the West seems to be a "playboy," a "womanizer," with a rough temper and debauchery. Even though Bethune volunteered to go to Spain for the anti-Fascist civil war from the winter of 1936 to June 1937, where he made remarkable achievements, he was still not regarded as a hero by his countrymen and even comrades, instead he had conflicts with his comrades in the same trenches to the point of inextricable tension and was sent back to Canada.

However, as the proverb goes, "An eagle sometimes flies lower than a chicken, but a chicken can never fly as high as an eagle." Even at the time when the Canadian public opinion disparaged Bethune to a very low level, they could not deny his outstanding medical skill. And in the phrase that "he was constantly perfecting his skill," Chairman Mao thoroughly explained Bethune's professionalism. His admiration that "Comrade Bethune's spirit, his utter devotion to others without any thought of self, was shown in his great sense of responsibility in his work and his great warm-heartedness towards all comrades and the people" thoroughly portrays Bethune's personality. Chairman Mao was really Bethune's true confidant!

At the 2019 symposium, I shared a personal experience with the participants to illustrate the Chinese grassroots people's interpretation of Bethune. Before the Qingming Festival in 2008, I followed Zhang Baotian, a retired Beijing office worker known as Lao Pu on the Internet, to a mountain village called Ganhejing in Yixian County of Hebei Province. Ganhejing was home to one of the sub-medical centers of the Communist Party-led Eighth Route Army's rear hospital at the anti-Japanese base of the

Shanxi-Chahar-Hebei border area during the War of Resistance Against Japanese Aggression. Dr. Bethune was on an inspection tour of these medical centers before he would return to Canada to raise fund for the Eighth Route Army in late October of 1939, which took him to Ganhejing. On the very day of his planned departure, October 20, 1939, the Japanese army launched a massive offense at the Eighth Route Army at Huangtuling, the Yellow Earth Ridge. And Bethune decided to postpone his journey home and went up north. In a small temple at Sunjiazhuang Village, a relatively safe place that could not be closer to the battle field, he made up an emergency surgery room and performed operations on wounded soldiers delivered from the battle front.

In this temple operation room, Bethune and his Chinese colleagues performed emergency operations on more than 40 wounded soldiers within 24 hours. It was during one of these operations that Bethune had a cut on a finger in his left hand, and got further infected while doing more operations on wounded soldiers when he later returned to Ganhejing. Then he learned about Japanese troops' new maneuver on November 5, and he rejected all the persuasions for him to retreat but went back to a village only 5 kilometers away from the battle front. At the time Dr. Bethune was running fever and very weak, but he still demanded that soldiers wounded at chest and head must be sent to him for examination.

Only at the order from Commander Nie Rongzhen did Bethune agree to retreat to the rear hospital. Yet his conditions had worsened so that he could hardly get up when he got to Huangshikou Village in Tangxian County, only 6 kilometers short of the hospital, on November 10. He stayed in the village and died there on November 12, at the age of 49.

Lao Pu drew a map illustrating the route Bethune took in his last ten days. He pointed out that Bethune actually took a zigzag track in this trip, because after he got infected, he still tried to go back to the front when he learned there was another battle. The zigzag route and the last track of his life were really heart-breaking. This road map clearly indicates Bethune's dedication to treating the wounded of the Eighth Route Army. This is the strongest sonata of nobility forged by the symphony of life.

Decades later, Bethune's greatness was finally recognized in his homeland. But many people trace his greatness to the "spirit of Christ" and believe that his greatness stemmed from the cultivation of the Christian spirit that he had received since childhood. After all, three generations up, Bethune's father and grandfather were both pastors.

We cannot deny the possible influence of the family's traditional religious belief on Bethune. However, until the mid-1930s when Bethune went to Spain and China to participate in the anti-Fascist war, people at that time did not consider him a great man except for his superb medical skills. If Bethune's greatness originated in the Christian spirit, then where was the spirit when he was described as "playboy" and "womanizer"?

Mr. Larry Hannant, a authoritative historian on Bethune studies in Canada, had a comment that impressed me deeply. He said that normally people are radical when they are young, and they tend to appease more and more as they get older. Bethune, as an exception, became more radical when he got older. He turned to Communism in 1935, when he was 45 years old. In that year, Bethune joined the Communist Party of Canada.

We should say that Dr. Bethune had his pursuit since childhood and was never mediocre. This was the basis for him to be a great man. Before going to Spain, he made himself an epitaph: "Born a bourgeoisie, died a communist." That's really extraordinary. Bethune also flourished in Spain, but his impact there was far less than what he made in China.

How comes that the same Bethune returned from Spain low, but went to glory in China? I think it was because Bethune met the Communist Party of China and the Eighth Route Army under its leadership. Although the CPC and its army were rustic, they were broad minded. This Party and its army respected him from top to bottom, but they never flattered him; they took care of him but never indulged him; and they managed to give full play to his talents while disciplining him. And the purpose and strategy of this Party and its army as well as the way they behaved also won Bethune's respect and convinced him. So he lived poor and happy in this land. His stinky temper that caused him troubles with his comrades in Spain did not have any unpleasant consequences in China. Bethune's stinky temper was still there, but he got along well with the Chinese comrades because the rustic army could overwhelm him. In the end, it was the Communist Party of China and the Eighth Route Army that ultimately led Bethune to greatness, and Bethune eventually sublimated into a noble and pure person in China and became part of the glorious tradition of our Party and our army.

Of course, not to forget Bethune's Communist belief does not mean that we have to put ideology on lips all the time. We are now talking about building a community with a shared future for mankind, in fact, Bethune was a pioneer of practicing the construction of such a community. Therefore, his greatness can transcend the times and get accepted and praised by all good-natured people; and the nobility he forged with the symphony of life can always echo in our hearts.

Xiong Lei

Witten at Muxidi, Beijing

June 16, 2022

心香一掬敬忠魂

汉英双语版长诗《纪念白求恩：格雷文赫斯特抒怀》就要出版面世了，希望读者能够喜欢。这是一首作者倾注了深情的叙事长诗，如同一道亮丽彩虹，架起人类友谊的桥梁，更是联结不同肤色和人种的崇高伟大心灵的交融通道。愿年轻的一代能喜欢这一曲跨越时空的福音。

十五年前，那个枫叶燃红的日子，我有幸带队赴加拿大考察农业。借此机会，终于圆了拜谒白求恩故乡的梦。格雷文赫斯特，一个陌生却格外亲切的地方，在那红枫林中美丽的古老小镇，我如愿以偿寻找到了自己心中敬仰已久的伟人故居，敬爱的白求恩医生梦开始的地方。我为之深深感动，甚至夜不能眠。我浮想联翩，热血沸腾，激情燃烧，化作创作灵感……于是写下了这首横跨时空的长诗。诗歌记录了白求恩的成长环境和人生轨迹，更是我情感燃烧的光焰放射。面对崇高精神的源头活水，想到生命高潮的惊涛骇浪……我为之惊叹，为之热烈鼓掌欢呼，更为之泪流满面。我为之庆幸，为之沉痛惋惜，更为之羞愧不已。感谢《中国作家》慧眼识珠，作为封面介绍的重点作品，完整发表全诗。更感谢中国读者的热情与强烈共鸣。随之而来的，就是希望国外读者能够了解诗中的激情、人物和感天动地的故事。感谢翻译家任小玫女士的精确诠译和辛苦劳作，使得我再度梦想成真。在这英汉对照版的《纪念白求恩：格雷文赫斯特抒怀》即将同读者见面之际，诚谢华艺出版社与北京燕山出版社同人的合作助力。此刻，我感到十二分的欣慰和幸福。假若白求恩大夫在天有灵，一定也会由衷高兴，因为这心灵歌唱的面世，意味着中国人民一直惦念着这位在我们困难中帮助过我们的老朋友。

我们每个人心中都有自己的英雄偶像。就像高山耸立在面前，更像是火炬于迷茫的至暗时刻，给我们以生存勇气和战胜困难的力量，导引我们人生前行的方向。这高山火炬，是我们心中耸立的灯

纪念白求恩

塔，无时无刻不提醒我们路应该怎么走，人生的意义究竟在哪里……我心目中的英雄偶像，他就是我从未见过面的，来自遥远加拿大的共产党党员：诺尔曼·白求恩。白求恩的确是一位天使，就像一朵祥云，他来自遥远的西方天际。原本过着安宁富足的日子，可他却冲着战火硝烟而来。那时候，中国人民抗日战争正是艰苦卓绝的相持阶段。白求恩自愿来到中国，帮助中国人民抗日的故事就像神话，在九州大地上流传。他在人们心目中是一个勇敢的战士，是一尊完美的医神，更是"一个高尚的人，一个纯粹的人，一个有道德的人，一个脱离了低级趣味的人，一个有益于人民的人"。（毛泽东语）这样的一个超凡的人，该是多么的可亲可爱，又是多么值得敬仰和纪念呀！从儿童时代起，夜晚当我一闭上眼睛，面前就会出现那个标志性的形象：高鼻子蓝眼睛，前额广阔无比的白求恩医生。他在一个孩子的心目中，是具体而又抽象的，是遥远而又亲近的。这就是精神偶像，就是必将影响我一生的楷模和榜样。这不是任何人强加给我的，而是潜移默化的自觉选择。那时候，时代英雄辈出。拿枪的不拿枪的，我却选择了这一位。从此一尊偶像耸立在心。令人高山仰止的白求恩：身材高大的一株参天大树，一个永远铭刻在心的伟大的名字。他那高大的身躯，弯腰在炮声隆隆的一座山神庙临时搭起的手术台前，给伤员做手术……的确是一尊永恒雕像，耸立在那里。他看着俨然是一位老人，胸前系着白围巾，袖子高高挽起，或是穿着短袖，一双有力的大手，动作灵巧又果断。他头发全白，双目锐利，神情严肃专注，就像天仙下凡一样……我正是从这幅定格在心灵深处的图像中，理解了"救死扶伤"的崇高含义。同样是外国人，当一些人举枪挥刀闯进我们的家园杀人放火的时候，他却自愿来到战场上，用自己的道义和精湛医术，挽救宝贵的生命……我出生在革命圣地延安。白求恩的故事就像延河清澈见底的流水和宝塔山上的悠悠白云之侧盘绕的雄鹰。他忘我工作的感人事迹，在我的幼小心灵中，铭刻下深深的烙印。那是影响了整整一个时代，渗透到几代人心灵深处的精神高标。那情景滋润和陶冶了几代人的心灵。一个外国人，毫不利己专门利人的动机……这是什么精神，这是国际主义的精神，这是共产主义的精神……小小少年，时常在梦中硝烟弥漫的战场上醒来，眼前就燃烧着一支火炬，照亮了黎明前的黑暗……这就是我的人生偶像，也是许许多多中国少年儿童效仿的典范。因为这个未曾见面却已经十分熟悉的人，他以自己的行动诠释了崇高的人生意义，他其实是用自己的牺牲奉献，把幸福的种子播撒到了我们的心田，最终必将形成一片红枫林，把中国和加拿大，以致整个世界连接起来，呈现红彤彤的一片温暖霞光。

忽培元

2022 年 1 月 29 日于北京

A Handful of Poetic Tribute Leaflets for the Loyal Soul, Norman Bethune

The bilingual long narrative poem *In Memory of Dr. Norman Bethune: A Pilgrim Tribute to Gravenhurst of Canada (Expressivo)* is going to press. I hope you should like it, in which has been concentrated all the truthful love of Norman Bethune, the hero of the poem. Not merely like a gorgeous rainbow building the bridge of friendship, it offers a panoramic view of communication endeavor between noble and great souls of all colors and races, which is earnest and energetic. May younger generation, whom I hope in particular, enjoy and benefit from the good message within, of international fraternity that carry through time and space.

It was in the autumn season of 2007 when maple leaves colored up like flaming fire fifteen years ago that I realized my long-cherished

dream of paying a visit to Gravenhurst, Norman
Bethune's hometown, while leading a survey
group to make agricultural investigation in
Canada—

This beautiful old town half-hidden among red
maple forests turned out at once strange and
familiar somehow. It saw my dream squared with
reality—finding the former residence of beloved
Dr. Bethune, the great man I have admired for a
long time, wherefrom his own life dreams began
to take flight. Right after the visit, it was
doomed to be a sleepless night for me, too
moved, immersed and lost in wild imagination. As
blood roused to a wave of flame, passion sparked
off flickers of illumination, brilliant poems
began welling up from the soul...Henceforth
expressivo in full swing, I composed this full-
length poem (i.e. the main text of this book),
which is supposed to made up of a score of
poetic pieces going back and forth in time and
space and recording the "microcosm" Bethune
grew up in and the trajectory of his life. This
suite of poetic tributes is an outpouring of my

overflowing heart.

Coming to face the matrix of his noble mental universe and think of stormy waves in his climax stage... I marveled at magnificence and glory of his life, warmly applauded and cheered for him, then burst into tears for a while. From time to time I rejoiced at his-toria, heaved a bitter sigh for him, and then more ashamed of the yawning gap between the idol protagonist and the humble I in reality. The whole output was accepted by *Chinese Writer* journal and published in 2018—as one of the key works recommended on the cover thanks to its discerning editorial board—which has appealed to the passion of and resonated with the Chinese readers ever since. What follows in future, to be expected, is the forthcoming understanding of the passion, characters and most affecting stories inherent in the poems on the part of foreign readership. Thanks to senior translator Ms. Ren Xiaomei's accurate interpretation and hard work, her English rendition boosted me to leak the secret dream and blow the dream bubble farther, like the big friendly giant (BFG for short) in Spielberg's awe-inspiring film again. Thanks also should go to the staff of Huayi Publishing House & Beijing Yanshan Publishing House, for their painstaking efforts and concerted support for this bilingual edition of *In Memory of Dr. Norman Bethune: A Pilgrim Tribute to Gravenhurst of Canada (Expressivo)*. At this moment, I felt an inexpressible relief, brimful of happiness. Dr. Bethune in heaven would also be heartily happy to see this, since the hymns springing from the bottom of my soul is an embodiment that the Chinese people have always been missing his honor, an old friend who helped us in hard times.

We all cherish our own heroes at heart, different heroic figures as tall as towering mountains ahead, or to be more exact, as soul-encouraging as torches lighting us through the darkest and most hazy moments, boosting us to re-spawn with mana points, to recover the ability and courage to survive and conquer all difficulties and keep on going along the directions of our life journey. Such a torch held aloft, is a beacon, a tower of light in our hearts, reminding us all the time how to go ahead and whereof the meaning of life is...

To be more specific, the heroic icon in my mind, as foretold, turns out to be Norman Bethune, a Communist whom came afar from Canada while I have never had any chance to meet at all. As a friend in need is a friend indeed, Dr. Bethune was a sort of angel, like an auspicious cloud fleeting from the distant Occident. He used to live a peaceful and prosperous life, but he came over to and for China, against the gun-smokes of war: At that time, the Chinese people were in notable exploits, fighting the difficult round to a lasting stalemate in the Resistance War Against Japanese Invasion. He voluntarily came to help the Chinese people in anti-Japanese endeavor. We treasured legendary tales about him and handed them down. Since then, he had been a valiant soldier, an Asclepius[1]-like médico divino, and more over "noble-minded and

1.God of Medicine among the ancient Greeks—Translator's note

pure, a man of moral integrity and above vulgar interests, a man who is of value to the people" (Mao Tse-tung) in our mind.

How amiable and lovely such an extraordinary person should be and deserve our credit, admiration and commemoration! When I was small, all I had to do was close my eyes for it to settle in front of me, the monumental image of Dr. Bethune in my mind's eye: a big-nosed, blue-eyed, and broad-foreheaded foreigner. He is at once concrete and abstract, distant and close for a child. As the idol, the model and exemplar, he illuminates a worshipper's whole lifetime naturally. That is not imposed by anyone, but a subtle pervasion of the spirit, without our being conscious of it. At that time, the revolution fever had bred heroes of the era one after another, with each mastering either the pen, the gun or anything else. As mentioned above, he was the one that I chose for admiration, a big fellow elevated as his character was, touching as was his story— Bethune, a stalwart figure, whose shining image is indelibly engraved on the memory of the people. In front of a makeshift operating table by the Mountain-God Temple, he proceeded assiduously with the operation in bent-down posture, with thuds of rumbling cannonballs right in his ears... All the while, he had stood by the operation table, like a Buddha statue. He looked an old guy with a white neckerchief on the chest, always either in rolled-up sleeves or wearing a short-sleeved shirt for the sake of convenience. Yet he was very deft, that medley of the big and strong hands' movement and gestures displayed how dexterous and decisive he could be. His hair was going completely gray and grizzled, his eyes were sharp. Solemn and focused, he's every inch like a deity on the earthly territory... His lofty image was frozen right there for me, perfectly interpreting the meaning of "healing the wounded and rescue the dying". While some foreign powers marched towards our home, committing murder, arson, and banditry, he volunteered to come from abroad to our battlefield instead. His saving many precious lives with superb medical skills has shown great generosity of spirit...

In Yan'an, the Cradle of Red Revolution where I
was born and bred, Yanhe River and Pagoda Mountain
were the most well-known. His life story was
as crystal clear to us like merrily gurgling
waters of Yanhe River. It was also high-soaring
in spirit like that of a widest-winged eagle
flying shoulder to shoulder with roaming clouds
above Pagoda Mountain. His unselfishness haunts
and infiltrates into the young soul of mine,
deeply imprinted there. The showcase represents
the high ground of nobility, which impacts a
whole era and carries profound implications
for future generations to come: stirring them
and filling the souls with gratitude as well
as uplifting their mind and spirit by way of
admiration. Behold & lo! What a foreigner! His
utter devotion had been made to others without
any thought of self...What is this spirit? This
is the spirit of internationalism, this is the
spirit of Communism...When I was a little boy, I
often woke up to see a flaming torch in front,
penetrating the dark mist before dawn, right

after breaking free from nightmarish scenario of battlegrounds thick with gunpowder fumes...

The torch figure—or to put it more precisely, the torchbearer—is not only the life idol on my own, but also a model (i.e. "apotheosis personality" in other words) for lots and lots of Chinese children: As for Bethune whom we have never met in person but been quite familiar with, his deeds spoke loud than others' words about the true greatness of life. We admire his sacrifice and dedication, which sowed the seeds of happiness into our hearts. From the minute saplings, they would ultimately grow into a patch of maple wood, bridging China and Canada, and casting a warm and radiant glow on the world canvas.

Hu Peiyuan

Written in Beijing,

January 29, 2022

目录

第一篇

Canto 01

圆梦

哪怕走过万水千山，

也要造访这偏远，

又平静的小城。

只为那一腔感动，

一个心底埋藏许久的梦……

枫叶红透的季节，

迎着清爽和煦之风，

行进在火红的林中。

眼前即亮起，

那一盏火红火红的灯。

Dream Squared with Reality

O, it's worth crossing thousands of rills and hills,

For the sake of asymptote,

To make a visit to this town, quiet and remote—

As a result of touching sentiments within,

And for a dream perpetual in my heart...

In the season when maple leaves turn flaming,

Basking a mild breeze,

I walk along the forest fiery-red;

While in front,

Out comes a ruddy glare to denote.

纪念白求恩

六十年后，

我们来了，

带来了中国人民，

万分感激之情。

六十年前，

一个平凡而伟大的生命，

那当过轮船侍者、

伐木工、

新闻记者、

小学教员

和医学学士的上尉医生，

Sixty years later,

Here we the delegation come,

With gratitude of the Chinese people

Which we cannot fully express.

Sixty years ago,

A man, humble and great in infinity like a mote,

Once worked as a civilian ship-waiter,

A lumberjack,

A journalist,

A primary school teacher,

Also as a military captain with a medical bachelor's degree.

纪念白求恩

似乎一切都干过了，

都成为这次远行的铺垫。

饱尝一切的艰难，

聚集燃烧的能源，

为完成一个生命，

最后的圣典。

To all walks of life he did devote,

All of which foreshadowed the forthcoming Odyssey.

Life's vicissitudes he experienced, at maximum,

Zealously gathering energy, or I say, momentum,

For the ultimate plunge in life,

I.e. chirping forth a swan-song canon of dictum.

第二篇

Canto 02

红枫

他不远万里地来了，

一位加拿大共产党员。

英国皇家外科医学博士、

美国胸外科高级会员、

联邦和地方政府卫生顾问，

这些荣誉和头衔，

一个也不留恋。

只以热情与生命，

伸张人间正义；

Red-Maple

From the other side of the world he came to our China—

A communist of Canada,

A Fellow of the Royal College of Surgeons in England,

An AATS[1] member in rank alpha,

A health consultant, both federal and local.

All these honors and titles, many an insignia or regalia,

He'd never been too spellbound to part with.

Only with his own life as well as mania,

He allowed justice to take its course;

---

1. the American Association for Thoracic Surgery—Translator's note

11

纪念白求恩

只以无私的援助，

保卫世界和平。

毛泽东的延安会晤，

那享誉世界的一次长谈，

还有《纪念白求恩》，

言辞恳切的美文，

成为外交佳话，

聚敛中华深情。

Only with selfless assistance,

Would he safeguard peace in a world of Utopia.

The meeting with Mao Zedong at Yan'an,

Their world-famous long talk,

As well as the memorial essay "In Memory of Bethune",

Such an eloquence brimful of sincere words,

That became a much-told diplomatic saga,

Amassing a wealth of devotion to China.

纪念白求恩

于是，

人们都说，

那神圣的火种，

是采自红星照耀的中国，

那不尽的能源，

则来自秋霜酿艳的红枫……

Henceforth,

All people say in nostalgia that

The single sacred spark

Comes also from China under the Red Star[2] ,

The endless stamina

Is pumped from maples reddened by autumn frost...

2.Bethune admitted early influence of Edgar Snow (1905-1972, American journalist and author who produced the most important Western reporting on the Communist movement in China), the new book-length report on the Chinese Communists *Red Star Over China* (1937) remaining a primary source on the early history of their movement in the world at that time.—Translator's note

第三篇

Canto 03

烈火

您是一团烈火，

点燃了就无法熄灭的火种。

您是一柄利剑，

舞起来就不会停止的剑锋。

圣火越过黄河，

利剑舞遍太行。

从此啊，

一支加美医疗队，

在战火硝烟中闪现。

Raging-Flame

O, what a gush of fire—no, a ball of flames for certain,

The one ne'er extinguished once ignited.

What a sharp sword,

That won't stop brandishing once pulled out of scabbard.

The sacred fire was to cross the Yellow River,

The swordplay was all over the Taihang terrain:

Under you, the captain,

A Canadian-American medical team,

Sped like a flash of silver amid smoke of war.

纪念白求恩

"改进随军医疗，

加强战地救助"，

"降低伤员死亡，

全力避免残疾"。

村头老槐树下，

田野庵棚间，

老乡土炕头上，

山神庙神龛前，

活跃着远道而来的您，

忙碌着高鼻蓝眼的神医。

"To improve medical treatment of marching armies,

As well as reinforce first aid in field rescue, not in vain",

"To reduce mortality rate of the wounded,

As well as spare no efforts to avoid disability".

Under old locust trees at the end of villages, on the strain,

In scrubby shack-sheds amid open fields,

On the warmer end of villagers' loess *kangs*[3] ,

Just before shrines, beneath eaves of mountain-god temples,

You went to great lengths from afar, time and again,

The bustling doctor, with a high-bridged nose and blue eyes.

---

3. stove-bed, an integrated system for cooking, sleeping, domestic heating and ventilation in north China—Translator's note

只要经您伸手，

死神定会吓走，

只要经您指点，

生命的火焰定能在，

将熄的躯体中复燃。

您的那一双大手，

实在是奇而又奇，

一时被传为，

战争死神的天敌。

A helping hand as long as you stretched out,

Grim Reaper itself will be baffled away.

Instructive directions as long as you did give or explain,

The flame of life will be carried on,

Rekindled in the dying body.

As for yours big hands, for certain

So miraculously sinewy they were

That in legends they told of highly skilled labor,

Betokening a valiant defender against the Death-in-War Villain.

第四篇

Canto 04

光 热

"把军区后方医院，

建设为模范阵地"，

亲手制作医疗器械，

亲自给医务人员授课，

编写医疗图解手册，

举办医务干部实习，

组织战地流动医疗队，

为减少伤员痛苦和残疾，

把手术台设在离火线更近，

更近的区域……

Radiance of Light and Heat

"As for military base hospitals,

To build them into models of renown",

He went in for it, making on his own medical appliances,

Teaching medical staff in person,

Compiling illustrated medical manuals,

Offering medical interns field-practice credentials,

Also running mobile medical units in the battlefield,

Setting operation tables closer to full-blown frontline,

To ease the travail,

And to reduce disability rate of the injured...

纪念白求恩

连续工作六十九个小时，

为百余名伤员治疗，

破天荒成立志愿输血队，

带头把鲜血献给重伤员⋯⋯

四个月啊，

战火中穿行的您，

行程一千五百公里，

做手术三百一十五例，

建立手术室、

包扎所十三处，

救治伤员千余⋯⋯

He worked around the clock, 69 hours in a run,

To treat over a hundred wounded soldiers.

First time ever in human annals,

A voluntary blood transfusion team he set up,

And took the lead in donating blood to those critically

wounded...

It was in four months,

That you trudged across barbed wires,

Twisting your way over 1500 kilometers.

A total of 315 operation cases he performed,

13 operating rooms and dressing stations he put up or knocked

together,

More than 1000 wounded patients he treated...

　　"一个战地医生，

　　同时要做木匠，

　　还要做缝纫能手、

　　铁匠和理发师。"

　　多功能的角色，

　　您是真正做到了的。

　　您用简单的工具，

　　把圆木锯开创平，

　　做成全世界绝无仅有的，

　　"卢沟桥"药驮，

　　像一个神奇的聚宝箱，

　　百余套手术器具，

"A doctor in action,

Was meant to be a carpenter,

And also a sewing expert,

A blacksmith and a hairdresser at the same time."

An all-round role,

You played smartly:

With simple tools,

You could saw and planed the log nimbly,

Shown by the unique Lugouqiao medicine pack in the world,

Which is virtually a magic "treasure trunk",

With over a hundred sets of surgical instrument,

五百个处方的药品，

统统在里面收藏。

还有那个，

精致的靠背架，

让术后的伤员，

依靠着呼吸锻炼。

骨折牵引架、

康复木床、

正骨夹板、

铁皮器皿，

还有精美的，

镊、钳、探针，

床被褥枕……

And supply for half a thousand medical treatment,

Were all stowed within.

In addition, the exquisite back-rest frame,

Was designed for convalescents after operation,

To lean against while doing breathing exercises.

And also bone-fracture traction,

Wooden sickbeds for rehabilitation,

Bone-setting splints,

Iron sheet hardware,

As well as the exquisite,

To name a few of it, forceps, pincers, probes,

Quilts, bedclothes and pillows...

第五篇

Canto 05

雕 像

您日夜操劳，

严重缺乏营养，

四十多岁的年纪，

英俊悄然被苍老代替。

前额的头发纷纷逃离，

露出亮而宽阔的阵地，

还有深深犁沟，

犹若新开垦的土地。

在抗日军民眼里，

Walking Buddha-Like Statue

Both locusts, of the day-and-night work strain

And the "cacotrophia", *i.e.* serious malnutrition,

Had eaten the prime of this former handsome guy

Of over two score years of age,

Who was stealthily turned into a shaggy pouch of skeleton.

A strand of hair fled off the forehead collectively,

Leaving behind a possie bright and broad position,

Deeply furrowed,

Just like a newly reclaimed land yon, beyond horizon.

In the eyes of the Anti-Japanese army men and civilians,

纪念白求恩

一座活雕塑挺立着，

那英武与高大，

都是无与伦比。

在故乡人们心里，

一株巨枫生长着，

一年一度的秋霜，

可爱的枫叶被染得火红。

A walking-Buddha sculpture stood upright,

So valiant and lofty,

Defying all comparison.

In the hearts of his native hometown,

A giant maple tree grows up.

Each year, in autumn frost,

Lovely maple leaves are tinted crimson.

第六篇

Canto 06

故乡

那是太行山的深秋，

枫叶又一度红透。

炮火连天的世界，

连天的炮火，

无法阻止英雄的脚步。

天空布满阴霾，

您思念故乡的苍穹。

放飞一只心灵的信鸽，

跨过强盗的阵地，

和雄伟无比的长城，

Hometown(s)

In Taihang Mountains, it was late fall,

When once and again maple leaves were hued scarlet overall.

It was the world where gunfire licked the heaven.

However, gunfire volleying which there might be,

Would never intimidate the hero into a standstill.

At the sight of haze-laden sky,

You missed the azure of your native town.

Like letting off a carrier pigeon from the innermost,

Your meandering thoughts flew over the border occupied by bandits,

And the majestically impressive Great Wall,

纪念白求恩

越洋过海，

飞往遥远的天边……

草地上的小屋，

还有祖父的摇椅、

父亲主持的教堂

与母亲温暖的亲昵。

清晨熟悉的炊烟，

黄昏安详的彩云，

微笑着的风……

您以逐渐麻木的双手，

捧一颗赤子之心。

Crossing oceans and seas,

And then to and beyond the distant horizon...

There was the cottage perched on the lawn,

The rocking chair of his Grandpa,

The church presided by his Daddy

As well as warm intimacy his dear Mommy did impart.

Cooking smoke at dawn so familiar,

Clouds crowned with dusk splendor so serene,

Breezes as warm as a smile...

On palms gradually numbed,

You proffered your heart in utter innocence.

纪念白求恩

那是树上飘落的，

第一片红透的枫叶，

贴在心坎上，

小心地在记忆中收藏。

化脓的手指，

疼得入骨钻心。

双腿已经不能站立，

手岂能操刀行医？

不能亲临前沿，

甚至不能查房询诊……

这是最大的痛苦，

感到自己已经无用。

The first blade of red maple

Falling from the tree, a carry-all,

Was pasted closer to your bosom,

And cherished carefully in memory.

Alas, purulent fingers

Were throbbing, painful to the marrow.

On legs you could not put yourself up,

How did you manage to hold the lancet, and as usual, carry all?

You could not go to the front in person

Or make daily visits to patients or wards...

That brought forth the pain, one sharpest and long-drawn:

The thought of being a useless guy.

纪念白求恩

躺在紧靠前线的地方，

万分思念亲人……

啊，安大略，

格雷文赫斯特，

重伤倒下的游子，

多么渴望故乡。

Lying close to the frontline,

He missed utmost his family...

Alas, Gravenhurst of Ontario,

One could never tell,

For a wanderer badly wounded,

How much he longed for his hometown.

第七篇

Canto 07

魂牵

您的故乡终于到了，

小镇是多么的安详。

瞧那老人、

那老枫树，

还有那狭窄的老街、

木屋、教堂。

梦境在这里凝固，

岁月的雕刻刀，

把不该留下的，

一切都剔除掉啦，

Dreamland Embarking

Your hometown I arrive at last—

What a peaceful whistle-stop townlet!

Behold! The senior citizen,

The old maple tree,

As well as the ancient narrow street,

The wooden manse, and the church.

Here the dream has been cemented solid:

By time,

All that should not be left over

Has been chiseled off,

只剩下奇妙与美好，

一幅迷人的木刻浮雕。

那亲切的形象，

装扮着眼前的路标。

那是在太行，

摄影家吴印咸的杰作。

一束如期而至的光芒，

把黄昏的灰暗照亮。

也正是那一瞬，

凝结了整个世界的目光。

Leaving only those miraculous and wondrous intact—

What a charming wood-relief picture.

With a friendly image of his own,

Road signs are inlaid with:

That well-known photo was shot in Taihang Mountains,

By a photograph master Wu Yinxian[4] ,

In which a beam of light, as if propitiously scheduled,

Lighted up the grey shades at sundown.

O it is the right "moment"

Which the whole world fix their eyes upon.

---

4. Wu Yinxian (1900-1994 吴印咸): a famous photographer and art director who studied in the Shanghai Fine Arts Junior College Army, head of the Film Group of the General Political Department of the Yan'an Eighth Route Army 1938-1946 and later on technical department head and deputy studio director of the North-East Film Studio in China—Translator's note

在东方您的第二故乡，

十多亿人，

熟悉的脸庞。

深邃无比的眼睛，

开阔无限的前额，

几道深刻的褶皱，

记录着岁月沧桑。

如今那座教堂——

父亲一生的搭档，

钟声依旧和蔼悠扬：

"要去人们，

最需要的地方。"

To more than one billion people,

In your second hometown, of the Orient,

What a familiar face it has been.

Les yeux profonds,

Forehead as broad as daylight,

Lined with a few deep furrows,

Recording the vicissitudes of time.

Nowadays the bells of the church

In his father's life-long service

Ring on, warm and melodiously:

"Lad, go to the right place

Wherefore thou are needed most."

父亲的嘱托，

像钟声一样洪亮。

阳光与微风，

代表母亲的慈祥，

将远方的朋友簇拥。

老枫树抖擞起精神，

红叶沙沙歌唱。

并不衰老的小屋，

依然蹲在那里，

目不转睛朝来客张望。

飘然而至的金发姑娘，

天仙般美丽动人。

The tenet of his father's admonition rings

As loud and clear as that bell toll.

Warm sunshine and gentle breezes,

On behalf of his Mommy's kind intuition,

Cluster round friends from afar.

The old maple tree perks up,

Its red leaves rustle.

The vicarage cabin is aged in years but not feeble at all.

It still squats there,

Gazing intently at visitors.

The blonde girl coming toward us with graceful manner

Looks as beautiful as a fairy full-grown.

纪念白求恩

这里早已辟为纪念地，

联邦政府出资，

购买了这座老房。

金发碧眼的讲解员，

热情地接待我们，

一再用中国话讲：

"你们是白求恩的老乡。"

For long it has been set up as a memorial site;

The old residence was purchased

Under the name of the federal government.

The guide with golden hair and blue eyes,

Hosts us warmly, crowning her greeting

With Chinese words in a repetitive tune,

"You guys are fellows of Bethune."

第八篇

Canto 08

忘我

炮火连天啊，

连天炮火的太行。

正义与邪恶，

殊死搏斗的疆场。

您为断腿的战士清理枪伤，

竟然被碎骨把手指扎伤。

您是医学专家，

深知病毒的可怕，

但却忽略了自己，

只关注战士安危。

Selflessness

Licking the heaven the gunfire was,

The gunfire was licking the heaven in Taihang,

Where justice and evil

Struck the fatal fight in a prang.

While cleaning up gunshot wounds for a leg-broken soldier,

By whose shattered bone, you got an incised finger wound.

As a medical expert you knew well the horror of virus,

But you chose to neglect and pushed it aside,

Focusing only on the safety of soldiers instead.

又一名伤员告急，

再度奋不顾身。

只想着戴手套操作，

会影响灵敏和效率。

等到隐患排除，

罪恶的病毒，

却侵入你积劳的躯体。

什么叫"毫不利己"？

什么叫临危不惧？

用善良与信念，

驱除罪恶与危机！

Another patient was hurried in, wounded and in emergency,

You dashed ahead, regardless of personal safety once again,

What you minded was only that, in case

Rubber gloves affect finger dexterity and work efficiency.

Potential dangers for patients were wiped out,

But venomous virus

Had invaded into your worn-out body.

What is "self-denial, *i.e.* utter devotion with no thought of self"?

What is fearlessness in face of danger?

With kindness and faith

You drove away evil in moments of crisis!

纪念白求恩

您心中那一团烈火，

把自己烧成通红。

昏天黑地里，

就像一盏明灯，

引领着白衣天使，

同死神抗争。

战斗紧张的时刻，

日寇炮弹在身边爆炸。

伤员过多的时候，

您忘记了寝食。

Flames in your heart

Makes you feverish and flushing.

In the darkness,

Like a guiding star,

Doctors and nurses, "angels in white", you were eager

To lead, in order to fight against death.

In moments of intense fighting,

Japanese shells exploded around, at close ranges.

When it was brimful of the wounded,

You got so involved, skipping sleep and meal.

纪念白求恩

什么血肉之体，

早已是铁铸的机器。

枪炮交响，

伤员呻吟，

您昼夜兼程，

与魔鬼搏斗。

每一次种下生之希望，

都在为烈焰加油。

进击、进击，

誓如鸣镝！

Oh no, that's not a body of flesh and blood anymore

But a running machine made of iron and steel.

Against background music bristled with many a gun and cannon,

Was symphonic groaning of the wounded.

You fought against the devil

Day and night at full speed.

Each time hopes of life you planted,

That fuelled the flame to be burnt to your cinder.

"Advance on, advance on",

The pledge twanged loud like a darting arrowhead!

纪念白求恩

在那一瞬间，

人们吃惊地发现，

平日和蔼可亲的您

果然化作了利剑：

小小的手术刀，

如同飞机大炮，

对准邪恶与罪犯

痛击，痛击，痛击！

At that moment,

People were surprised to find that

You the mild

Turned into a sharp sword outspread:

The small scalpel,

In a giant plane or bombarding cannon style,

Scored the bull's eye at evils and criminals,

Trouncing hard, hard, hard!

第九篇

Canto 09

孤寂

眼下并非战斗间隙，

您却感到了孤寂。

您躺在荒山坡上，

手指红肿得像枫叶的颜色，

幻化成故乡的记忆。

为了前线药物募集，

您刚刚往返大洋。

妻子已经离异，

父亲撒手人寰，

唯有年迈的母亲，

Solitude

At present, it was not an interval between battles;

Yet you felt embedded in solitude.

While crouching on a barren hill,

Turgid and rigid fingers, as reddish as maple leaves,

Dozed you off, into nostalgic fantasies of the hometown:

To raise fund for drugs in demand for the frontline,

You went back and forth across the Ocean on errand.

As a divorcee, you countermanded matrimony,

Meanwhile dear Dad had passed away,

Only your old Mom saw you off

送您重返前线。

分手的那一刻

老人家目光湿润，

默默无语……

临行到爷爷坟前跪拜，

曾把一片孝心敬献。

那是来自长城的枫叶，

经历过战火硝烟的洗礼，

同故乡的枫叶一样艳丽，

寄托着无尽思念。

To be back to the grilling frontline.

At the moment of parting,

The old guy's eyes were moist,

Though no goodwill words she uttered from the lips...

Right before the moment of departing,

You prostrated before Grandpa's grave stock-still

As a token of love and filial devotion.

That blade of maple leaf from the Great Wall,

Trudging through the baptism of war first-hand

Retained its red color, as bright as those of your native land,

Embodying ceaseless missing and yearning.

第十篇

Canto 10

亲人

眼下，

我们来了，

格雷文赫斯特。

替您看望那些，

您所熟悉的亲人。

那安眠在枫树林中的父母，

还有最爱您，

对您影响最大的，

足智多谋的祖父。

Kinsfolk Beloved

Right now

Here we are,

Gravenhurst!

To pay a visit on your behalf to all those

Family members you knew well.

Among the maple forest are your parents—in eternal stay—,

And your resourceful grandfather

Who loved you most,

The greatest influence on you who had swayed.

纪念白求恩

带着太行山的卵石，

摆成一个心形的花圈，

献在老爷爷的墓前。

也替您在草地上，

捡几片可爱的红枫叶，

这虔诚的举止，

感动了金发姑娘。

她的眼里聚满了泪水。

"请进，

请进。"

我们随她进入，

Pebbles of Taihang Mountains far-away,

We lay out in a heart-shaped wreath style,

In front of Grandpa's grave.

Also a few lovely red maple leaves are to be picked up,

In lieu of you, from the turf straightaway.

This endeavor, so pious and wishful,

Played upon the blonde guide's heart the music of ripples,

That a flood of tears welled up in her eyes.

"Come in, please,

Come in, please."

We followed her in,

您出生的小屋，

如今已是博物馆的展室。

那里有许多，

您童年的照片，

还有父亲、

母亲、

爷爷同您一起的合影。

有一张湖畔戏水的小照，

是儿时活泼又可爱的您。

面对这张珍贵图片，

想到您太行山裸泳的片段。

人们伫足不前流连忘返，

Into the vicarage cottage where you were born,

Now one of the museum's exhibition sections.

There are many pictures,

Of your childhood,

And also of your father,

Mother,

Grandfather and you.

In a small photo you were playing water by the lake—

Without suspicion what an adorable and lovely boy!

The sight of this precious picture,

Reminds us of your swimming naked in Taihang Mountains.

Visitors stop for a pause, there and then linger on,

仿佛同您一道，

回顾着美好童年。

人们最同情的，

是您的婚姻情感，

阴差阳错的结合，

使两人共同遭难。

合了分分了又合，

彼此无论怎样努力，

上帝无法撮合，

无缘的心灵干涸。

As if to be in company with you,

Looking back on the childhood, good old days.

What arouses most sympathy is

Your love and marriage life—

A nuptial union of odd coincidence

Enthralled both spouses into a marathon of suffering:

You two married, separated midway, reunited.

Anyway, despite all painstaking efforts,

You two, God could not fix it up or bring together—

If not predestined, souls would part company, part ways.

第十一篇

Canto 11

自强

可怕的肺结核，

曾经使您绝望，

自暴自弃的态度，

曾使您失去生活勇气。

沉沦中您坚强地

站立起来，

还有什么恶魔，

不可战胜！

多伦多医学院，

Self-Improvement

Terrible tuberculosis,

Once dragged you into the abyss of despair,

Self-abandoning attitude,

Once impaired you, depriving the courage to live on.

Instead of sinking into depravity,

You pulled yourself together resolutely.

Would there be a devil

Invincible? Not at all!

What a rare, brilliant student

难得的高才生啊，

同学中有多少，

学者、

专家和总统。

那一长串名单中，

谁也没有超过您，

为人类赢得殊荣。

"一位具有，

国际影响力的英雄"，

加拿大政府，

曾如此替您命名。

Of University of Toronto (Medical College),

In a hall of fame for alumna,

There would be a long name-list of

Distinguished scholars,

Gurus and presidents,

But unsurpassable new surprise you are, undoubtedly,

In winning a great honor

For the whole mankind.

"The hero, one who wins

International distinction",

The Canadian government

Once claimed your worth with such a citation.

您的果敢行动，

常人难以置信。

几乎完美的结局，

证明了出类超群。

勇敢奔赴西班牙，

参加反法西斯斗争，

创造性地实践：

发明流动输血车的，

战地医生。

蒙特利尔供职五年，

您发明三十余种医疗器械，

Your bold behavior, courageous action,

Are always beyond belief for the laic.

A marvelous, almost perfect finale,

Proved your accredited superiority.

You bravely rushed to Spain,

Committing yourself to the anti-Fascist campaign,

Ingeniously creative in medical practition:

What an angelic doctor you were in war—

Inventing the mobile blood-transfusion lorry!

During the five-year service in Montreal,

Over thirty medical devices you invented,

至今人们还在使用，

以您命名的肋骨钳。

您性格内向，

不苟言谈，

对世俗不屑一顾，

整天埋头钻研，

每篇不同凡响的论文，

皆是守旧者眼中之钉……

Among which rib-cutting forceps named after you

Nowadays are still in use.

Introverted,

Reticent,

Not caring a damn about the worldly,

You studied all day long.

Each outstanding paper you wrote

Turned out to be an eyesore to the conservative headstrong...

第十二篇

Canto 12

奉献

炮火连天，

连天的炮火，

您奋勇直前。

"不能再近了，

这里太危险！"

"什么危险、

危险，

战士在火线上拼命，

我们怕什么危险！"

Dedication

Gunfire licked the heaven.

Despite gunfire that bombarded the heaven hard

You marched forward.

"Do not be any closer.

It's too dangerous here!"

"What hazard,

Hazard,

Should we be afraid of

When desperate soldiers are fighting hard at the front?"

三天三夜，

连续在手术台上奋战，

直到结束战斗。

您自称"万能输血者"，

刚刚拔掉与伤员，

连通的输血管，

又拿出母亲带给您的，

荷兰纯牛乳，

亲自到厨房烧煮，

再精心烤好馒头片，

端到重伤员面前。

For three days and three nights,

You stationed at the operating-table foothold nonstop

Until the end of the battle.

Self-claiming a "universal blood-bank guy".

Upon pulling out blood transfusion tube

Between you and the wounded,

You took out a tin of Holland condensed milk

That your mom had hoarded atop in luggage,

And went to the kitchen to heat it,

Then you put a tray of steamed bread slices baked carefully

In front of the severely wounded guy.

"趁热儿，

快吃吧，

勇敢的孩子！"

伤员吃着，

感动落泪。

您疲惫的微笑，

像父亲一样慈祥。

"Before it turns cold,

Gobble on the fly,

Brave kiddo!"

The patient was moved, tears shedding

As he dug in the food onward.

Your smiling face which looked somewhat haggard

Was as kind as that of a standard Old Daddy in his eyes.

第十三篇

Canto 13

战士

如今啊，

故乡的人们，

深深为您骄傲。

您是人类的荣誉，

以短暂的人生，

揭示了生命的真谛：

永远告诫人们，

不要拘泥于名利。

战士自有战士的风采，

Fighting Warrior

Nowadays,

Fellows of your hometown

Take pride in you.

In the glory of human beings,

You revealed the true meaning of life

With your short lifespan tableau:

Always warn people against,

Possible confinements of the celebrity or parvenu.

Soldiers have their own graceful bearings.

红枫的本质啊，

无私无畏，

坦诚绚丽。

再高贵的苍蝇，

毕竟只是苍蝇，

倒下去的战士，

永在人间挺立。

您的故乡为您自豪，

来自中国的朋友，

被视为兄弟。

我们受到贵宾的待遇，

By nature, red maple,

Is an incarnation, by which selfless and fearless,

Frank and brilliant qualities shine thru.

No matter how noble a fly is,

It is only a fly after all.

Among the world, a fallen warrior will

Forever stand upright on the plateau.

Your hometown is proud of you.

We, friends from China,

Are treated like brethren.

As distinguished guests,

纪念白求恩

连您父亲的书屋，

您出生的卧室，

都允许进入参观致意。

这在早先并不曾开放，

我们感到无比荣光。

您安眠在大洋那边，

巍峨的太行怀抱之中。

必然是梦中常回故乡，

难怪过去了这么多年，

人们还如此把您思念。

Even your father's book study

And the bedroom in which you were born,

We're priviledged to pay a visit to.

Since both are not open to a regular visitor,

Tremendously honored we did feel.

Across oceans, eternal slumber you sank into,

In the embrace of Taihang Mountains.

In dreams you must have been back home many times.

No wonder so intensely people here miss you,

Even if for years you had been out of their familiar purlieu.

第十四篇

Canto 14

思念

1939 年 11 月这天，

太行山经霜的枫叶，

如同血染。

战争尚未停息，

依旧炮火连天。

白大夫想要重返前线，

才发现自己双脚，

已经瘫痪。

瞅着肿胀变形的左手，

接下来将发生什么灾难？

Yearning

On that day of November, 1939

Frosty maple leaves of Taihang Mountains

Were turning as bloody as one could imagine.

The war was not over,

Gunfire were still raging beyond the skyline.

Eager to return to the front line,

Dr Bethune mere found out that

His lower limbs were paralyzed.

Examining the swollen, deformed left hand,

He knew not what would happen next.

纪念白求恩

他咬紧牙关，

为自己切开伤口，

强忍疼痛把脓血挤走。

这是最后的一搏，

为了告别的时刻。

脑海中就像电影，

不断浮现出，

激动人心的场面。

临别之前，

您很想再见一次毛主席，

听他分析战局，

谈笑共勉。

With his teeth clenching,

To cut the wound open himself he determined,

Squeezing the pus away in pain.

This tuned out to be his fatal fight,

Before the deadline for everlasting farewell.

Memories fleeted like a motion picture in his mind,

With exciting scenarios constantly recurring in outline.

Before time was up for the Final Judgment ,

How eager you were to see Chairman Mao again,

Listening to his analysis of war aff airs,

Talking and laughing together in mutual encouragement.

纪念白求恩

您想回一趟故乡，

探望父母和爷爷，

能像一个真正的中国人，

在亲人坟头燃一炷高香。

同时，

向当地党组织，

汇报这里的情况……

How you longed to get back to your hometown,

Paying a visit to your parents and grandfather,

And "doing what the Romans do", *i.e.*

Burning Chinese incense on the graves of the beloved.

At the same time,

You wrote to report current affairs here,

To the affiliated Party organization…

纪念白求恩

想到要处理自己的物品，

想到了亲切的聂司令员。

于是他强忍痛苦，

提笔写下了，

感天动地的遗言。

At the thought of disposing personal belongings,

At the thought of dear Nie, the Commander[5],

The last words he scribbled down

—so touching as to move the Heaven—

While bearing bravely the long-drawn pain on his own.

---

5. Nie Rongzhen (1899-1992 聂荣臻): a Chinese Communist military leader who joined the Communist Party in 1923, went to Moscow for military study, returned to China for the revolutionary cause all along. At the founding ceremony of the People's Republic of China on October 1st, 1949, General Nie led four divisions of troops past the reviewing stand. —Translator's note

Canto 15

纪念白求恩

遗言

"亲爱的聂司令员:

今天我感觉非常不好,

也许我会和你永别了!

请你给布克写一封信,

地址是加拿大,

多伦多城威灵顿街 10 号。

并将同样的内容,

写给国际援华委员会

和加拿大民主和平联盟会。

Last Words

"DEAR COMMANDER NIE:

I feel very low today.

Maybe I shall bid adieu to you evermore!

Please write a letter to Buck[6]

—Whose address is 10 Wellington Street,

Toronto, Canada—I implore.

And also copy the letter content

For the China Aid Council

And the Canadian Democratic Peace Alliance as before.

---

6. T.B. (Tim Buck,1891-1973), one of the Canadian Communist Party founders, then acting as General Secretary of the Party. —Translator's note

告诉他们吧，

我在这里十分快乐，

我唯一的希望就是——

就是能多有贡献。

也写信给，

美国共产党总书记，

并寄上一把日本指挥刀

和一把中国大砍刀，

报告他们吧，

我在这边工作的情形。

把我所有的相片、

日记、

文件，

Tell them

That heretofore I have been very happy.

My only regret is—

That I shall not be able to do more any longer.

Also please write to

General Secretary of the American Communist Party,

Along with my Japanese samurai sword

And a Chinese machete.

Brief them

The inns and outs of my work here.

All my photos,

Diaries,

Narratives

纪念白求恩

一概寄回那边，

由布克负责分散。

并告诉他这里，

也已是一片枫叶红艳……

有一部电影片子即将拍完。

将我永不改变的友爱，

送给所有我的，

加拿大和美国的同志！

两个行军床，

你和聂夫人留下吧。

两双英国皮鞋，

也留给你穿。

Will be mailed back there,

For store and at the dispersal of Buck.

And inform him of

This land hued with maple-leaf redness already...

A motion picture which will be completed soon[7].

Give my everlasting friendship and love

To all of my comrades yore,

Both in Canada and America!

My two camp cots,

Are for you and Mrs. Nie [Madame Zhang Ruihua].

My two pairs of British leather shoes

Also go to you.

---

7. "No motion picture ever arrived."(Source: Ted Allan and Sydney Gordon, *The Scapel, the Sword: The Story of Doctor Norman Bethune,* McCleland and Stewart Limited, 1971, p311 n1)—Translator's note

骑马的马靴和马裤，

给冀中区的吕司令员。

贺师长也要赠一些纪念品，

给军区卫生部长两个箱子，

游副部长十八种手术器械，

林医生可以拿十五种，

卫生学校的江校长让他，

任意挑选两种物品作纪念……"

写到这里，

您已经泪流满面。

My riding boots and breeches

I should like to give Commander Lv of the central Hebei district.

Division Commander He can select whatever he pleases as a memento.

My two cases should be given to Sanitary Service director of our

military region.

Of my surgical instruments, Vice-minister You is to have eighteen,

Therefore Dr. Lin galore, another fifteen.

Jiang, Medical School principal,

May choose two as souvenir of solace..."

While knitting up to this point,

You found unceasing tears bathing your face.

第十六篇

Canto 16

战友

这些亲切的名字，

亲切的面容，

多么熟悉的朋友，

生死与共的同志、

战友。

真舍不得与大家分手，

紧握的手怎么能，

说丢就丢。

"给我的勤务员邵一平

Comrades-in-Arms

All these genial names,

Cordial faces,

Such familiar friends,

Comrades fighting through thick and thin together,

Comrade-in-arms.

You hated to part with everybody.

How can friends' hands be let loose

Once getting clenched?

"I would like to give each blanket

To Shao Yiping, my attendant

和炊事员老张头，

每人一床毯子，

并送给邵一平，

一双日本皮鞋。"

啜泣使您周身颤抖，

只得又一次停下笔，

任泪水扑扑倾流。

"每年要买250磅奎宁，

和300磅的铁剂，

专为疟疾患者

和极大数目的，

贫血病患者预备。

And my cook Zhang the Oldie.

A pair of Japanese-made leather shoes.

Should also go to Shao."

Sobbing made your body tremble,

So you had to pause again,

Letting tears dripping down.

"Each year, we need to get ready

250 pounds of quinine

And 300 pounds of chalybeate

For malaria patients

And a huge number of anemia patients.

千万不要再往保定、

天津一带购买药品，

那边的价钱，

比沪港贵两倍。"

讲到了医务工作，

您便有更多的放不下。

这也担忧，

那也恐怕，

几乎忘记了自己的眼下。

一阵更加剧烈的疼痛，

使您几乎昏迷。

Never buy medicine in such cities as Baoding,

And Tientsin again,

Since prices offered there were much higher

Than those of Shanghai and Hongkong, by twofold."

Furthermore, about medical work,

You were too worried to let go of—

Thoughts of this matter you cared about

And that one you were concerned with,

Almost blinded you from your own situation.

A sudden pang, more poignant,

Almost knocked you out.

纪念白求恩

"告诉加拿大和美国，

我十分的快乐，

我唯一的希望，

是能够多有贡献。

最近两年在中国，

是我平生最愉快、

最有意义的时日。

我不能再写下去了……"

您无奈地松开笔，

静静闭上了眼睛。

"Tell the guys of Canada and the United States that

I have been very happy.

My only hope is

That I shall be able to make further contribution.

The last two years in China

Have been the happiest and most splendid years

Of my lifetime.

I'm afraid I'm too invalid to write more..."

Reluctantly you loosened grip on the fountain pen in midair,

Shuttering quietly the flickering eyelids.

第十七篇

Canto 17

祈祷

六十年之后，

我们走进您父亲——

牧师工作的教堂，

默默地为您祈祷。

我们深知，

无神论者的您，

并不指望上帝能够灵验。

但在这静谧的空间，

更适于人们把您怀念。

In Prayer

Almost threescore years later,

We walk into the church

Which your father serviced with as a minister

And pray for you in silence.

Keenly we are aware of you,

In atheist inclination,

Who never expected God's omnipotence.

But it is serene and quiet here,

Suitable enough for lament in mourning performance.

纪念白求恩

这显然是小镇上，

年龄最长的建筑，

精美的穹顶刚刚翻修，

老房子显得精神异常。

就像您记忆中的，

祖父和父亲的模样。

父亲当年在这里工作，

从小屋到教堂，

每日总要往返几趟。

在侧门的石阶上，

我们俯下身，

抚摩那凝固的时光。

In this town proper,

Obviously it boasts the oldest building in appearance,

With an exquisite dome in renovated elegance.

And the whole ancient complex looks

As exceptional in lusty radiance

As ordained grandfather and father

In your treasured memory at a nostalgic glance.

Your father used to work here.

From the hut to the church,

He went back and forth several times a day.

On stone steps of its side entrance,

We stooped

To touch the trail of frozen time.

纪念白求恩

父亲的容貌，

同儿子十分相像，

只是留着唇髯，

神情威严异常。

父亲的威严

与母亲的慈祥，

爷爷的智慧与爱，

簇拥着您的成长。

离开小镇的时候，

您才懂得什么叫故乡。

"Like father, like son"—

Your father's complexion was a master copy in semblance,

Except for his beard

And dignified countenance.

With the awe-inspiring ambience of your father,

The benevolent caring of your mother,

And the wisdom and love of your grandfather,

You were blessed to grow up from adolescence.

Only after leaving the townlet,

Did you come to catch what "hometown" meant.

第十八篇

Canto 18

神医

炮火连天啊，

连天炮火的战场，

您率领"东征医疗队"，

深入冀中前线。

什么"铁壁合围"，

什么"冬季扫荡"，

这样那样的鬼名堂，

您同中国军民视若家常。

一口气工作69个小时，

给115名伤员连续手术。

Médico Divino

Gunfire licked the heaven.

Amid gun-firing and bombarding beyond the horizon,

You led "the medical team of Eastward Expedition"

Deeper into military action of central Hebei Province.

The enemy's dirty tricks like "encirclement of iron walls"

Or monkey business like "winter sweeps",

You—as well as the Chinese people, civilian or in army—

Brushed away as none other than trivial.

Working around the clock for 69 hours,

Operating on 115 patients without a break,

纪念白求恩

世界医疗史上的奇迹，

恐怕是后人永远无法破译。

1939 年 10 月，

您已经周身浮肿，

疼痛难忍，

还坚决要求去战地救护，

"白大夫呀，你不能不要命！"

"你们不要拿我当古董，

要拿我当一挺机关枪使用。"

Credited you a wonder in world medical-treatment history,

Which I'm afraid none will decipher in future therewithal.

In October1939,

Despite swollen all over,

Suffering from unbearable pains,

You insisted on going for first aid in the battlefield.

"Dr. Bai[8], it would be suicidal to risk going there!"

"Don't treat me like an exquisite antique,

Take me medial, as a machine gun."

8.That is surely not a play upon the word by the poet himself: It turned out that Dr. Bethune was mistaken for Dr. Bai due to the difference between Chinese and Canadian names: The surname Bethune sounds like a full name (B-E T-H-U-N-E) in the Chinese naming system, in which the family name happens to be placed before the given name, to those who love him deeply in Taihang Mountains. Hence the endearment. —Translator's note

纪念白求恩

在战斗的间隙里，

您同太行人民，

建立起深厚友谊。

人们亲切地唤您大叔，

那亲如一家的关系，

时刻感动着您。

您成了人们心中的神医，

"药到病除"，

被人们传得离奇。

您有空还为邻居，

挑水扫院，

During fight intervals,

You had established profoundly congenial friendship

With the Taihang people.

They call you "Uncle" cordially,

The family-like intimacy

Always touched you at heart.

You were lauded as a saga—a miracle-working doctor

"Once whose medicines play, symptoms will be away"—

Too legendary to be true in reality.

In spare time

You carried water

And swept the courtyard for neighbors.

纪念白求恩

说自己是一个真正的八路，

要遵守三大纪律，

八项注意。

土法上马制作的，

"卢沟桥"驮子，

如今就陈列在，

家乡的博物馆里。

Since to be an Eighth Route Army man both in word and action,

One should abide by "the Three Main Rules of Disciplines

and Eight Points for Attention"[9] .

The Lugouqiao piggyback,

An ingenious device inspired by local wisdom,

Is on perennial display

In the special museum of his hometown.

9.regulations promulgated for implementation in the Chinese people's army—
Translator's note

第十九篇

Canto 19

想您

穿什么，

住怎样的房屋，

盖怎样的棉被，

冀中在哪里，

雁北又有什么圣迹……

有许多许多的稀奇，

您的同胞和

乡亲们极感兴趣。

金发姑娘是讲解，

更像是采访一样，

Missing You

What you was clad in,

What kind of shelter you took residence in,

What kind of cotton quilt covered you for the night,

On earth where is central Hebei Province,

What famous sites there are in Yanbei area...

There are manifold livelihood details

That compatriots and villagers of your homestead

Are curious for knowing reassurance.

The blonde girl is a professional guide in the main,

But this time more in an interviewer mood instead,

问了我们许多问题。

她一边问，

一边还在速记，

神情格外着迷。

您在中国的故事，

多么富于魅力，

轰轰烈烈像风，

点点滴滴似雨。

您的和蔼可亲，

您的幽默风趣，

刀刻斧砍一般，

铭记在我们心间。

Popping up a lot of questions.

While making endless inquiries,

Shorthand she is also taking

And seems quite charmed in utterrance.

Your life story in China,

How fascinating it was by nature,

So vigorous like a gust,

So fine like drizzling rain in dribs and drabs, as is understood.

Your amiable compliance,

Your sense of amusement and humor,

Have been inscribed and hewn in clear lines

Upon our hearts.

您是多么透明，

儿童般的天真。

几十天没能洗澡，

您会脱得精光站在雨里。

负伤的战士在您面前，

就是至高无上的上帝。

您于手术台旁昏倒又站起，

脸上仍聚满笑意。

还有与老乡们的交际，

如同八路军元帅，

将军们与您的友谊……

What a crystalline and innocent mind

You are endowed with.

After dozens of bathless days,

You never miss the rejoice of standing naked like a new-born in

the rain,

A wounded soldier was, in your brain scheme,

Somewhat a sublime messenger consigned from the Above.

After swooning at the foot of operating table,

You sustained to stand up, keeping smiles all over the face

domain.

As regards your social networking with fellow villagers,

Your genial friendship with marshals,

And with generals of the Eighth Route Army...

纪念白求恩

您的故乡的人们，

想知道您的一切，

您的故乡的人们，

早把您尊奉心中。

像多伦多巍峨高塔，

像洛基山峻峭雪峰，

不，您在人们的心中，

只是这格雷文赫斯特，

美丽小镇上一棵巨枫，

春绿夏艳秋红，

四季歌唱人生。

People in your hometown

Fain gain knowledge of everything about you.

People in your hometown

Have taken you as an idol of worship for a long time.

Like the majestic tower of Toronto,

Like steep snow peaks of Rocky Mountains,

Oh, no, in people's hearts,

You are none other than a giant maple

In the beautiful townlet of Gravenhurst—

Outbursting green in spring, bright in summer and red in

autumn,

Chanting the psalm-of-life quartet melody all year round.

纪念白求恩

春天，

人们由您的萌芽，

感受生命的蓬勃；

夏日，

人们从您的脚下，

体会绿荫的清凉；

秋季，

您化作了一团烈火，

照耀幸福的大路。

冬季，

您如哲人，

In springtime,

People catch the vigor of life

From your sprouting reckless;

In summer,

People get the cool of green shade

When walking under your canopy;

In autumn,

You turn into a gust of bright fire

Shining on the road to happiness;

In winter,

You are like a philosopher,

深思中给人以宽慰。

人们只要同您亲近，

就可以品味出甜蜜。

您以生命的交响，

回答着什么是高尚。

您以牺牲奋斗的榜样，

注释着生活的意义。

难怪您的基碑，

能被地球托起。

Giving solace by means of deep meditation yearly.

Sweetness shall be flavored

As long as they get acquaintance with you.

By the symphony of life

You show "What is nobility?" in response.

By showcasing sacrifice and struggle of a devotee

You elucidate the meaning of life.

No wonder your monument will be

Vouchsafed up on the globe.

第二十篇

Canto 20

诞生

金发姑娘的眼神，

透着思念的忧伤；

金发姑娘的表情，

折射着千百万人的惆怅。

在信念危机的十字街头，

人类将走向何方？

让我们一道儿，

在您出生的床前，

合个影吧。

黑头发与黄头发交织，

共同感受一下，

母与子的安逸。

Birth Reveries

The eyes of the blonde girl

Are full of nostalgic sadness;

The complexion of the blonde girl

Whistles the melancholic note of millions of people.

In the crossroads of belief crisis,

In which direction will mankind head for?

Let us guys hurdle closer to the bedside,

Right near where you were born,

And take a session picture,

To mark the event that the dark and golden haired mingle

To feel and share coziness between Mommy and Sonny.

当您诞生的那一天，

阳光也该是同样明媚。

窗外同样有鸟鸣风吟，

也有树影婆娑。

一切都悄然平静，

衬托出您的啼声。

男丁稀少的牧师家庭，

领略了上帝的荣耀。

那情形就像，

在反扫荡的途中，

您为早产的农妇接生……

It must have been, when you were born,

Another bright and sunny day,

With stray birds twittering out of the window,

And trees casting fluttering shadows in the same vein.

All is quiet, for certain,

To set off your first cries in the world.

The Reverend family—with rare odds of a boy offspring—

Were immersed in glory of God for His special favor,

Somehow as if to be foretold

Of your bold delivery of a peasant woman's premature baby

On a march to repulse the enemy's "mopping up" campaign. [10]

10.What a coincidence that his surname was translated as 白 (the White) 求 (seeking) 恩 (grace) in Chinese.—Translator's note

第二十一篇

Canto 21

告别

"亲爱的人们啊,

不要难过……

大家,

努力吧,

向着伟大的路,

开辟……

前面的伟大。"

告别的时刻到来,

永恒的生命,

将以另一种形式存在。

Farewell-Bidding

"Dear fellows,

Don't be sad...

Everybody,

Try hard,

To blaze for

The great road...

Greatness ahead."

When the time to bid farewell comes,

Eternal life would take shape

In another form overhead.

纪念白求恩

人们难免忧伤，

人们不胜惆怅。

难忘您最后的嘱托，

那复杂心情旁人难以想象。

您投身炮火连天的战场，

是做好了牺牲一切的准备。

这一走意味着什么，您不能不预想；

这一去何时归来，您不能不思量。

纵使太行山的劲风，

使您变得更加坚强，

毕竟您也不是铁石心肠。

People were sad inevitably,

People were weighed down with melancholy.

We shall never forget your last bequest,

Made in a complicated mood unimaginable.

You had been ready to yield to everything

When throwing yourself afield despite the volley of gunfire.

You could not but help anticipating

What the forthcoming departure would suggest.

You could not but help pondering over

When to be disbanded home again later on.

Even if strong blasts of Taihang Mountains made you more

forbearing,

After all you were bland by nature to sum up.

纪念白求恩

您是否在告别那一刻，

情不自禁地洒过热泪？

您是否在离去那一刻，

遥拜过这一片，

生您养您的热土？

Did you ever cannot help shedding tears

At the moment to say goodbye?

Did you ever pay remote worship to it

At the moment to leave the remote land

Where you had been born and raised up?

第二十二篇

Canto 22

相 拥

红枫树的根，

深植此地，

火一般的烈焰，

温暖着世界。

一个生命的热量，

究竟有多少大卡？

又能够创造，

怎样的奇迹？

美丽的金发姑娘，

她无从告知，

我们当然也无法考据。

In Embrace

Like a red maple,

Deeply rooted here

Like a roaring flame

Warming the world beyond the healing extension.

How many calories

Can a life afford to burn off?

What kind of miracles

Can be worked out by such a champion?

The beautiful blonde,

Has no way to tell us,

And surely we have no research resort either.

纪念白求恩

六十年后这一时刻，

诗人才真正体会到，

您生命的威力。

难道是您的魂魄，

已经附体，

难道是您的精神，

更加积极。

我突然感到了一阵心悸，

大滴大滴的泪珠，

滚落在生您养您的土地。

这情感早已把金发姑娘感动，

她突然伸开双臂，

Till this lingering moment, sixty years later,

I, the poet, come nearer to realize your divine life-power in

ecstasy.

Am I not soul-possessed in precession,

Or by virtue of your spirit

Boosted to be more positive?

A fit of palpitation I suddenly sink into,

Big tear drops rolling down

To the land where you had been born, raised up.

At sight of this emotional fusion,

The girl in blonde coloring, deeply touched for long,

Suddenly stretches out her arms

把我紧紧拥入怀里。

就在那神圣的一刻，

彼此离别的瞬间，

黑头发与黄头发的我们，

都把对方假设成了您……

我们拥抱得很紧很紧，

生怕一旦松手，

就会失之交臂。

拥抱的人儿久久不愿松开，

就像替您拥抱日夜思念的，

乡土与母仪。

为您而相互拥抱的人们，

And hugs me around tightly.

On that sacred occasion,

The time for farewell,

We, dark haired and blond haired

Take each other to be you in trancing confusion...

We hug very tightly,

For fear that once letting go of,

By a narrow chance, the other would be doomed to abandon.

We hug for a long time, too reluctant to stop,

Just like hugging, on your part,whom you missed day and night,

Both the land and the paragon of motherhood.

we, in embrace on your behalf,

纪念白求恩

彼此能听到对方的心音。

能感到满腔热血的澎湃，

能感知您心胸有多宽广，

能掂出那心灵，

无私跳动的分量，

能明白什么是崇高伟大，

能领略"具有国际影响力"的您，

对于人类精神的未来导向。

2018 年 2 月 6 日

全文发表于《中国作家》

Can hear each other's heartbeat,

Pulse passionate surging of blood,

Feel how broad-minded you are,

Figure out the weight of your heart in aeon—

By virtue of its selflessly pounding, *homo sapiens* thereon

Are empowered to understand what is sublimity and greatness,

To fathom future orientation of human spirit

Via ye, the pillar of salt with "international distinction".

(Inspired by true events,

full Chinese text published in *Chinese Writer* journal

on February 6, 2018)

◦白求恩赴华后主要活动◦

纪念白求恩

1937 年 7 月 30 日

白求恩参加美国洛杉矶医疗局举行的欢迎"西班牙人民之友"宴会，遇到了中华全国各界救国联合会领导人之一的陶行知。陶行知向白求恩介绍了"七七事变"后中国的抗日战争形势，白求恩向陶行知表示："如果需要，我愿意到中国去！"白求恩就此事向加拿大共产党作了汇报，称"西班牙和中国都是同一场战争中的一部分""中国比西班牙更加迫切需要医生"，"（白求恩）在西班牙的经验可以运用于中国的反法西斯战场"。

1937 年 12 月

受美共与加共的派遣，白求恩赴纽约接受国际援华委员会（由共产国际授意美共与加共推动组建，配合宋庆龄主持的保卫中国大同盟为援华抗日做募捐宣传）资助组建了加美医疗队准备赴华从事战地医疗工作。该医疗队的另外两人是：北温尼伯的圣约瑟夫医院外科手术医疗部的精通中文的加拿大籍女护士简·伊文（Jean Ewen，或译作琼·尤恩，中文名于青莲）。临行前参加的美国外科医生帕森斯。

1938 年 1 月 8 日

加美医疗队携带一批药品和手术器材，从温哥华乘船乘坐"亚洲皇后"号邮轮赴中国。登船前白求恩给前妻弗朗西斯写了告别信。"西班牙是我心头的一块伤疤……西班牙和中国为同一目的而战斗。我去中国，因为那儿最需要我，在那儿我可以发挥更大的作用。"

1938 年 1 月 20 日—2 月中旬

抵达香港，收到了美国共产党中国局让八路军驻香港办事处负责人廖承志安排加美医疗队乘飞机至武汉的通知。在武汉等待北上期间，经史沫特莱协调，周恩来派王炳南去接头后与博古亲切接见了白求恩一行。白求恩与伊文到汉阳基督教长老会医院（今武汉市第五医院）帮助工作；医生帕森斯决定留在武汉国统区，白求恩明确拒绝了在蒋中正所领导的国民政府管辖区工作，转而帮助中国共产党。

1938 年 2 月 22 日

经过周恩来安排，白求恩与伊文押送医疗物资的数十辆大车离开武汉，经战乱中的河南、陕西潼关渡黄河到山西风陵渡、运城，至临汾附近的八路军总部。这时遇到日军沿同蒲铁路南下进攻。（3 月 3 日在山西河津，他度过了在中国的第一个生日即 48 岁生日。）

1938 年 3 月 20 日

白求恩一行又经潼关转道抵达西安。

1938 年 3 月 31 日

在八路军驻西安办事处负责人林伯渠的安排下，最终抵达延安。受到各界的热烈欢迎，并很快结识了先于他来到延安的美国医生马海德和共产国际派驻中国的军事情报员李德。

1938 年 4 月 1 日

与毛泽东会面时，白求恩说利用他从北美带来的医疗器械足以组建一支战地医疗队，到前线就近抢救重伤员；毛泽东对白求恩说的伤员立即手术将有 75% 的复原率很高兴，表示会大力支持他的工作。

1938 年 4—6 月

由延安出发，渡过了黄河，越过了重山，冲破了敌人
的封锁线，于 6 月间顺利到达晋察冀军区。认识了比
他晚来五台山几天的美国驻华武官卡尔逊（访问抗日
根据地的第一个美国政府代表、第一个外国军事观察
家），并在晋察冀军区军政干部学校作报告。

1938 年 5—7 月

和从汉口请假赶来的基督教传教士查德·布朗医生一
直搭档工作。

1938 年 6 月 18 日

由晋察冀军区卫生部部长叶青山陪同，赶赴 30 公里
外的军区后方医院。医院的 520 多名伤病员分别住在
五台县松岩口村及其附近的河西村、河北村。白求恩
先用一周时间对全部伤病员逐个进行了检查，然后用
四周时间为 147 名伤员做了手术，其中包括平型关战
斗中负重伤尚未痊愈的一一五师伤员。

1938 年 8 月 7 日

白求恩到金刚库村向聂荣臻当面提出，建立一个起示范作用的模范医院，以便培养医务人员。聂荣臻同叶青山商量后，同意了白求恩的意见，确定在军区后方医院第二所的基础上改建。白求恩非常高兴，在他的组织领导下，动员军队和地方群众的力量，开展了突击性的"五星期运动"。

1938 年 8 月下半月

赴冀西巡回医疗约两周，在阜平县龙泉关招提寺、曲阳县南家庄尔村、唐县军城等地，为部队的多名伤员做了手术。在曲阳县还热情动员凯瑟琳·霍尔（新西兰传教女牧师，中国名何明清），说服她以特殊身份出没于日寇占领区为八路军购买药材等。

1938 年 9 月中旬

模范医院在松岩口建成，15 日举行了落成典礼。聂荣臻和晋察冀边区政府领导人宋劭文、胡仁奎等出席，白求恩发表了热情洋溢的讲话。

1938 年 9 月 28 日

白求恩到达平山，首先在四分区后方医院，参加了洪子店战斗的救护工作，为数十名伤员进行了检查和手术，并帮助该院改进管理工作。以后参加了小觉镇妇救会庆祝胜利大会，还参加了洪子店四分区的祝捷大会，应邀在会上做了讲话。

1938 年 10 月 22 日

白求恩根据对四分区的巡视情况，给聂荣臻写了士兵优抚工作的建议书。

1938 年 10 月 25 日

白求恩到达观音堂乡花木村军区后方医院，看到医院的建设和工作方式，仍然保持了模范医院的传统与作风时，甚为高兴。其间，他还到秋卜洞、河口村、常峪村等地巡回医疗。先后为晋察冀军区参谋长唐延杰、我军众多的伤员和两名头部受伤的日军战俘做了手术，并给当地群众治病疗伤。

1938 年 10 月 29 日

白求恩由军区卫生部副部长游胜华陪同，到达军区司令部所在地平山蛟潭庄。聂荣臻向他们介绍了军区反"扫荡"形势后说："昨天三五九旅在广灵张家湾、邵家庄至灵丘贾庄的公路上，伏击日军独立第二混成旅团的战斗激战一天，歼敌常冈宽治少将以下500余人，我军伤员较多，王震旅长请白求恩率医疗队赴灵丘医治。"

1938 年 10 月 30 日

白求恩一行回到常峪村军区卫生部，着手组建西征医疗队。西征医疗队由白求恩和游胜华带领，队员中有翻译董越千、医生王道建、护士赵冲、勤务员何自新、炊事员冯志华等。

1938 年 11 月 6 日

医疗队整装出发，离开平山赴灵丘。

1938 年 12 月 7 日

白求恩在灵丘杨庄草拟了一份给聂荣臻的报告，建议在军区后方医院一所的基础上，成立特种外科医院。第二天与游胜华讨论修改后，用电报发出，很快得到聂荣臻的同意。

1938 年 12 月 15 日

白求恩在灵丘杨庄组建了"晋察冀军区特种外科医院"。按照白求恩的主张,医院成立了院务委员会,吸收各方面代表参加,包括伤员和村干部在内,实行民主管理。

1939 年 1 月 3 日

白求恩在晋察冀军区特种外科医院主持了"特种外科医院实习周"活动,训练团以下机构的卫生人员。第一批有第一、第三军分区和三五九旅的 23 人参加。学习结束后,白求恩给他们颁发了手写的实习合格证。

1939 年 1 月 13 日

北方分局第二次党代表大会在平山县北苍蝇沟召开……白求恩作为特邀代表参加了会议。

1939 年 1 月 16 日

到达三分区唐县花塔医院,用 10 天时间初步建立起第二个特种外科医院。然后返到涞源插箭岭军区后方医院，为在南、北石盆村战斗中的伤员施行了大小手术300多例。

1939年1月底

结束"西征"，回到平山军区卫生部。

1939年2月3日

参加边区党代表大会，在边区党代表大会上发言。

1939年2月7日

成立东征医疗队。

1939年2月15日

军区首长批准东征医疗队到冀中，白求恩离开平山赴冀中。

1939年2月19日

从定县清风店穿过敌人的封锁线进入冀中，21日到达冀中军区司令部。

1939 年 3 月 3 日

白求恩在冀中的战斗中度过了 49 岁生日,这一天他做了 19 例手术,直到第二天 6 点才休息。医疗队在冀中军区后方医院,一天内检查了 200 多个伤员,三天内实施手术 40 多例。后转到一二○师卫生部,当天施行手术 60 余例。

1939 年 3 月 14—5 月 18 日

白求恩率医疗队进行战场救护,前后经过了 4 次战斗:3 月 14—19 日,留韩村战斗;4 月 15 日,大团丁村战斗;4 月 26—28 日,齐会村战斗;5 月 18 日,宋家庄战斗。

1939 年 5 月初

白求恩还利用战斗空隙,到河间县四公村,检查了隐蔽在那里的八路军伤员。

1939 年 6 月

在冀中后方医院巡回医疗,开办医生、护士训练班,以提高医务人员业务水平。6 月 20 日,为军区卫生学校拟定了教育方针的文件。6 月 30 日，白求恩回到晋察冀军区卫生部。

1939 年 7 月

7 月 1 日，在完县神北村给聂荣臻、布克、白劳德、林可胜博士寄去了《加美流动医疗队四个月的工作报告》。12 天后在完县神北村完成 6000 余言的《关于改进卫生部门工作的建议》。此时，白求恩因腿部感染，转到唐县和家庄军区司令部休养，其间，编写了《游击战中师野战医院的组织和技术》一书。

1939 年 8 月 1 日

白求恩在和家庄写出《加美流动医疗队月报》。之后，完成了外科医生适用的《初步疗伤》《模范医院标准》等书籍和讲义。

1939 年 9 月

9 月初，白求恩伤愈回到花盆村卫生部，参加了军区卫生部长会议，对军区卫生部提出许多具体意见。9 月 18 日，白求恩在唐县牛眼沟村军区卫生学校开学典礼上讲话。同时提出组织军区卫生部视察团，视察并扶助各分区部队卫生工作的建议。9月25日，军区卫生部视察团由卫生部长叶青山带队，白求恩、后方医院院长林金亮等人参加，从花盆村军区卫生部出发。视察路线为：唐县于家寨，曲阳县南家庄尔村、郎家庄、灵山、党城、上河，唐县老姑村、葛公村，完县神南村、北清醒村，易县坎下、独乐、松山、管头。

1939 年 10 月 20 日

白求恩原定启程短暂回北美为组建八路军后方医院与晋察冀军区卫生学校筹款。这时遇上了日军发动对晋察冀冬季大扫荡。白求恩选择留下来参与反扫荡作战的医疗救治。

1939 年 10 月 29 日

涞源县摩天岭战斗中为一名腿部受重伤的伤员做手术，在日军迫近手术所时为加快手术进程，白求恩把左手伸进伤口掏取碎骨，一片碎骨刺破了白求恩的中指。

纪念白求恩

1939 年 11 月 1 日

白求恩为一名颈部患丹毒合并蜂窝织炎的伤员做手术，手指处的开放创口遭到感染。

1939 年 11 月 8—10 日

11 月 8 日，到达易县旺家台三团卫生队，体温已达 39.6℃。11 月 9 日，高烧至 40℃，剧冷、打寒战、呕吐，仍然坚持工作。11 月 10 日，白求恩病情加重，三团首长决定送他到军区后方医院救治，派担架往驻在唐县花盆村的军区外科医院护送。当日下午 3 时，路经唐县黄石口村时，白求恩决定在此停留，护送人员将其安置在村民邸俊星家的小北屋里住下。

1939 年 11 月 12 日

清晨 5 时 20 分因败血症在河北省唐县黄石口村农民邸俊星家去世。去世前一天写给聂荣臻的遗书：

亲爱的聂司令员：

今天我感觉身体非常不好，也许我要和你们永别了！请你给加拿大共产党总书记蒂姆·布克写一封信，地址是加拿大多伦多城威灵顿街10号，同时抄送国际援华委员会和加拿大民主和平联盟会。告诉他们，我在这里十分快乐，我唯一的希望就是多做贡献。

也要写信给美国共产党总书记白劳德，并寄上一把缴获的战刀。这些信可以用中文写成，寄到那边去翻译。随信把我的照片、日记、文件寄过去，由蒂姆·布克处置。所有这些东西都装在一个箱子里，用林赛先生送给我的那18美金作寄费。这个箱子必须很坚固，用皮带捆住锁好，外加三条绳子。将我永世不变的友爱送给蒂姆·布克以及所有我的加拿大和美国的朋友们。

请求国际援华委员会给我的离婚妻子坎贝尔夫人拨一笔生活款子，分期给也可以。我对她应负的责任很重，决不能因为没钱而把她遗弃了。还要告诉她，我是十分内疚的，并且曾经是快乐的。

两张行军床、两双英国皮鞋，你和聂夫人留用吧。马靴、马裤，请转交吕（正操）司令。贺（龙）将军，也要给他一些纪念品。

两个箱子给叶（青山）部长；18种器械给游副部长。

15种器械给杜医生；卫生学校的江校长，让他任

217

意挑选两种物品作纪念。

打字机和绷带给郎同志。手表和蚊帐给潘同志。

一箱子食品和文学书籍送给董同志,算我对他和他的夫人、孩子们的新年礼物。

给我的小鬼和炊事员每人一床毯子,另送小鬼一双日本皮鞋。照相机给沙飞。

贮水池等给摄影队。医学书籍和小闹钟给卫生学校。

每年要买250磅奎宁和300磅铁剂,用来治疗疟疾患者和贫血病患者。千万不要再到保定、天津一带去购买药品,那边的价钱要比沪、港贵两倍。

最近两年,是我平生最愉快、最有意义的日子。在这里,我还有很多话要对同志们说,可我不能再写下去了。让我把千百倍的谢忱送给你和千百万亲爱的同志们。

白求恩

1939 年 11 月 23 日

中共中央致电加拿大共产党中央委员会转白求恩医师家属称:"白医师突于本年 11 月 12 日,因施行手术

不慎，致中毒死于晋察冀边区。这是我们一个重大的
损失。"

朱德总司令、彭德怀副总司令致加美援华委员会转白
求恩大夫家属电称：白求恩大夫"于本年 11 月 12 日
于晋察冀边区逝世。敝军将士，闻此噩耗，莫不深为
哀痛！"

1939 年 12 月 1 日

举行了延安各界追悼白求恩大夫大会。大会致加美援
华委员会转白求恩大夫家属电称：白求恩大夫"不幸
于本年 11 月 12 日，因施行手术，致中毒殒命于晋察
冀边区，噩耗传来，全延安党政军民学各界人士，均
认为这是中华民族与全世界人民之重大损失，极表哀
痛，除举行追悼大会，并表扬劳绩外，特致慰问之意。"

1939 年 12 月 21 日

毛泽东为八路军政治部、卫生部将于 1940 年出版的
《诺尔曼·白求恩纪念册》专门写了一篇文章《学习
白求恩》（新中国成立后编入《毛泽东选集》第二卷
时题目改为众所周知的《纪念白求恩》）。文中说：

纪念白求恩

白求恩同志……不远万里，来到中国。……一个外国人，毫无利己的动机，把中国人民的解放事业当作他自己的事业，这是什么精神？这是国际主义的精神，这是共产主义的精神，每一个中国共产党员都要学习这种精神。……白求恩同志毫不利己专门利人的精神，表现在他对工作的极端的负责任，对同志对人民的极端的热忱。……从前线回来的人说到白求恩，没有一个不佩服，没有一个不为他的精神所感动。晋察冀边区的军民，凡亲身受过白求恩医生的治疗和亲眼看过白求恩医生的工作的，无不为之感动。……我们大家要学习他毫无自私自利之心的精神。从这点出发，就可以变为大有利于人民的人。一个人能力有大小，但只要有这点精神，就是一个高尚的人，一个纯粹的人，一个有道德的人，一个脱离了低级趣味的人，一个有益于人民的人。

Chronicles of Norman Bethune

in China (1937-1939)

纪念白求恩

July 30, 1937

At the banquet in honor of "Friends of the Spaniards" hosted by Los Angeles Medical Bureau, Norman Bethune met Tao Xingzhi (陶行知 1891-1946, one of the leaders of the All China Saving-the-Nation Federation), who introduced to him the austerity of the War of Resistance Against Japanese Aggression in China after the July 7th Incident. Bethune told Tao that if necessary he was willing to go to China! When reporting this to the Communist Party of Canada, he mentioned that "Spain and China are part of the same battle", "I'm going to China because I feel that is where need is greatest; that is where I can be most useful", and his "experiences in Spain... would be invaluable in China".[1]

1.Ted Allan and Sydney Gordon, *The Scalpel, the Sword: The Story of Dr. Norman Bethune*, Toronto, Canada: McClelland and Stewart Limited, p167, p167, p166.—Translator's note

December, 1937

Bethune was dispatched by the American
Communist Party and the Canadian Communist
Party to New York, where he got the support
of China Aid Council—an international
committee set up by the above two parties at
the instruction of Comintern (*i. e.* Communist
International) to cooperate with the China
Defense League headed by Mme Soong Qingling（宋
庆龄1890-1981,*aka* Madame Sun Yat-sen, widow of
the first president of the Chinese Republic）
in terms of fund-raising and publicity for the
aid to China's fight against the Japanese—
and set up a Canadian-American medical team to
go engaging in medical work at the battlefield
of China. The other members of the triad
were Jean Ewen（于青莲1911-1987, a Canadian
female nurse proficient in Chinese working in
surgical department of St. Joseph Hospital
at northern Winnipeg）and Charles Edward

纪念白求恩

Parsons (?-1940, an American surgeon hurriedly joining in right before the setting-off of the journey).

January 8, 1938

The trio left Vancouver on *Empress of Asia* for China, along with medicines, surgical equipment and supplies. Before coming on board, Bethune wrote a farewell note to his ex-wife, Frances Campbell Penny, "Spain is a scar on my heart...Spain and China are part of the same battle. I am going to China because I feel that is where the need is greatest; that is where I can be most useful." [2]

2.Ted Allan and Sydney Gordon, *The Scalpel, the Sword: The Story of Dr. Norman Bethune,* Toronto, Canada: McClelland and Stewart Limited, p167.—Translator's note

January 20 to mid-February 1938

Upon arrival in Hong Kong, the three of them received a notice from the Chinese Bureau of the American Communist Party, to the effect that Liao Chengzhi (廖承志 1908-1983, head of the Eighth Route Army's Hong Kong office) would arrange for the Canadian-American medical team's flight to Wuhan. While waiting to go north in Wuhan, they met with Zhou Enlai (周恩来 1898-1976, deputy director of the Political Department of the Military Commission stationed in Wuhan) and Bo Gu (博古 1907-1946, organization director of CPC's Yangtze River and South Bureaus) after the negotiations of Agnes Smedley (1892-1950, famous American reporter, writer, social activist) and the initial contact of Wang Bingnan (王炳南 1908-1988, publicity director of CPC's South Bureau) Bethune and Evan went to Hanyang Presbyterian Hospital (a

纪念白求恩

clinic run by the sisters of the Missionary Society of St. Columban in Hanyang according to another version, now Wuhan Fifth Hospital) to help their work. While Dr. Parsons decided to stay in the KMT-controlled Wuhan city, Bethune explicitly refused to work in the jurisdictions of the National Government headed by Chiang Kai-shek (蒋介石 1887-1975), and turned to help the Communist Party of China instead.

February 22, 1938
By virtue of the arrangements of Zhou Enlai, Bethune and Evan left Wuhan with dozens of heavy medical- supply loads. They trudged through Henan and waded across the Yellow River via Tongguan in Shaanxi during the turmoil of war to Fenglingdu and Yuncheng in Shanxi, and then on to the headquarters of the Eighth Route Army near Linfen. At that

time they encountered the Japanese south-bound attack while jogging along the Tongpu Railway. (Then it is noteworthy that he spent his first birthday in China, *i. e.* the 48th birthday, in Hejin County of Shanxi Province on March 3, 1938.)

March 20, 1938
Via Tongguan, Bethune and his team reached Xi'an.

March 31, 1938
Under the arrangements of Lin Boqu（林 伯 渠 1886-1960, head of the Eighth Route Army office in Xi'an). they arrived at Yan'an (the headquarters of the CPC) at last, where they were enthusiastically welcomed by local guys from all walks of life and stroke acquaintance with Shafick George Hatem（马海德 1910-1988, the first foreigner to join the Communist

纪念白求恩

Party of China who changed his name to Ma Haide in 1937) and Otto Braun (李 德 1900-1974, a Comintern agent sent to China from 1934 to 1939).

April 1, 1938
When meeting with Mao Tse-tung (毛泽东 1893-1976, leader of Chinese Communists), Bethune said that the medical equipment he brought from North America was enough to set up a field medical corp which could go straight to the front lines and rescue the critically wounded. Pleased to hear that 75 per cent of such cases would recover if operated immediately, Mao promised to throw his support behind Bethune's future work.

April to June, 1938
Afterwards he successfully reached the Shanxi-Hebei-Chahar military region in June, after

a bumpy journey from Yan'an, across the Yellow River, heavy mountains and the enemy's blockades. He met Evans Fordyce Carlson[3] (1896-1947, who arrived at Mount Wutai several days later on his nearly two-year inspection journey as an American observer of the Chinese armies, including nearly a year with guerrillas behind Japanese lines. He also made a speech at the Military and Political Cadre School of Shanxi-Chahar-Hebei military region.

May to July, 1938
He had been partnering with Dr. Richard Brown (1898-1963, nicknamed Chad, a young Canadian missionary attached to the Methodist Mission

---

3.the U.S. Marine officer during WWII leading guerrilla fighters—Carson's Raiders—on daring military incursions in the Pacific area, the first American government representative and also the first international military observant visiting Anti-Japanese base areas in China—Translator's note

纪念白求恩.

Hospital in Hankow) who turned up for medical
help on leave from Hankow.

June 18, 1938
Accompanied by Ye Qingshan (叶 青 山 1904-
1987), health minister of Shanxi-Chahar-
Hebei military region, he rushed to the rear
hospital of the said military region 30
kilometers away. It took Bethune a week to
make a medical tour, examining one by one over
520 patients of the hospital scattering around
in Songyankou Village of Wutai County as well
as Hexi Village and Hebei Village nearby. Then
he spent another four weeks on 147 operations,
including those wounded of the 115th Division
who had not recovered from heavy injuries
after the Pingxingguan battle.

August 7, 1938

Bethune went to Jingangku Village and proposed to Nie Rongzhen (聂荣臻 1899-1992, Commander of Shanxi-Chahar-Hebei military region) there and then that a model hospital be set up to train medical staff. After discussing and consulting with Ye, Nie agreed and decided to reconstruct the second base hospital of the military region into a model hospital. Bethune was very happy at that. Under his leadership, organization and mobilization, the military forces and local people launched the "Five-Weeks Campaign" for the rush project at a whirlwind pace.

The second half of August, 1938

He toured for medical treatment in western Hebei Province in a fortnight, and operated on many wounded soldiers at Zhaoti Temple in Longquanguan of Fuping County, in

Nanjiazhuanger Village of Quyang County and Juncheng of Tangxian County. While in Quyang, he also passionately talked Miss Kathleen Hall (何明清 1897-1970, a New Zealand sister) into playing an active role in going to Japanese occupation zone to purchase medical supplies for the Eighth Route Army.

Mid-September, 1938

The model hospital was inaugurated at Songyankou on the 15th. General Nie Rongzhen and leaders of the Shanxi-Chahar-Hebei border region government such as Song Shaowen (宋劭文 1910-1994) and Hu Renkui (胡仁奎 1901-1966) arrived for its opening ceremony, during which time Bethune delivered a passionate speech.

September 28, 1938

After arriving in Pingshan, Bethune threw himself into the Hongzidian Battle rescue work at the hospital behind the lines of the Fourth Subarea. He examined and operated on dozens of the wounded, and also helped advancing the hospital's administrative management. Later on, he attended the victory celebration meetings held by the Women's Salvation Association of Xiaojue Township and the Fourth Subarea of Hongzidian, at both of which he was invited to make a speech.

October 22, 1938

Based on his inspection of the Fourth Subarea, Bethune stated in his letter to Nie a proposal on preferential treatment of the war disabled.

October 25, 1938

When he arrived at the base hospital at Huamu Village, Guanyintang Township, Bethune was very happy to see that model hospital had been in much the same condition as before.

Meanwhile, he embarked on a tour of Qiubudong, Hekou Village, Changyu Village, etc. for a round of medical inspection. He performed surgeries for the wounded in action—among which Tang Yanjie（唐延杰 1909-1988, chief of staff of Shanxi-Chahar-Hebei military region), our army soldiers as well as two Japanese prisoners of war with head injuries, to name a few, and healed the wounded folks.

October 29, 1938

In company of You Shenghua（游 胜 华 1912-1996, vice health minister of the military region), Bethune jogged along the road to Jiaotanzhuang Village of Pingshan County, where the military region headquarters was stationed. After introducing the current anti-"mop-up" operation in the military region, Nie said that "The 359th Brigade ambushed the Japanese second independent mixed brigade on the highway from Zhangjiawan and Shaojiazhuang of Guangling to Jiazhuang of Lingqiu for a whole day yesterday. During the fierce battle, more than half a thousand enemies under Major General Tsuneoka Kanji (常冈宽治 1886-1948) were annihilated, while there were many casualties on our side as well. Brigade commander Wang Zhen (王 震 1908-1993) asked Bethune to lead the medical team to Lingqiu for medical cure. "

October 30, 1938
Bethune and his team returned to the health department of the military region at Changyu Village and started to set up a medical team for the western expedition, which was to be headed by Bethune and You Shenghua. Among the members were Dong Yueqian (董越千 translator), Wang Daojian (王道建 doctor), Zhao Chong (赵冲 nurse), He Zixin (何自新 attendant) and Feng

纪念白求恩

Zhihua（冯志华cook）, *et al.*

November 6, 1938
The medical team readied themselves and left Pingshan for Lingqiu.

December 7, 1938
Bethune drafted a report to Nie in Yangzhuang of Lingqiu County, proposing that a special surgery hospital be built on top of a hospital behind the lines of the military region. After discussing and amending it with You the next day, he sent the concerned report by telegram, which soon got Nie's approval.

December 15, 1938
The "Special Surgery Hospital of Shanxi-Chahar-Hebei military region" was built in Yangzhuang, Lingqiu. In pursuance of Bethune's proposal, the hospital set up a hospital

committee, which included representatives from all aspects—for example, the wounded within and local cadres of the village—to implement democratic management.

January 3, 1939

Bethune chaired the "Practical Work Week" program in the Special Surgery Hospital of Shanxi-Chahar-Hebei military region to train the health faculty of those units below the regiment. The trainees of their first session consisted of 23 members from the First Military Subarea, the Third Military Subarea and also the 359th Brigade. At the end of the training period, Bethune presented handwritten diplomas of qualified internship to the trainees.

January 13, 1939

The Second Party Congress of the North Branch

纪念白求恩

was held in Beicangyinggou, Pingshan County...
which Bethune attended upon invitation as a
special delegate.

January 16, 1939

The second special surgery hospital was
established in just 10 days, after he reached
Huata Hospital of Tangxian County. Then he
went back to the rear hospital of the military
region at Chajianling, Laiyuan County to
perform over 300 operations on those wounded
during the Nanshipen Village and Beishipen
Village battles.

End of January, 1939

After the end of the "western expedition",
he returned to the health department at
Pingshan.

February 3, 1939

He made a speech while attending the Party Congress of the border region.

February 7, 1939

A medical team of the eastern expedition was set up.

February 15, 1939

As the head of the military region approved action plan of the medical team for the eastern expedition, Bethune left Pingshan for central Hebei.

February 19, 1939

Braving through the blockade at Qingfengdian of Dingxian County into central Hebei, they arrived at the military headquarters of central Hebei on 21st of this month.

纪念白求恩

March 3, 1939

Bethune attained his 49th blessed birthday amidst the battle in central Hebei Province: In this special day, he performed altogether 19 operations, with no rest till 6 o' clock the next morning. On the whole, the medical team inspected over 200 wounded at the rear hospital of the Central Hebei military region in one day, and performed more than 40 operations in three successive days. And no less than 60 cases were operated right on that day after they transferred to the health department of the 120th Division.

March 14 to May 18, 1939

Bethune headed the team to carry out medical rescue of the four battles: first in Liuhan Village from March 14 to 19, second in Datuanding Village on April 15, third in Qihui Village from April 26 to 28 and the fourth in Songjiazhuang Village on May 18.

Early May, 1939

Employing the intervals of fighting, Bethune went to Sigong Village of Hejian County where he made medical checkup for the wounded Eighth Route Army men hiding there.

June 1939

In order to boost professionalism of medical staff, the touring medical service and training classes for both doctors and nurses were provided in rear hospitals of central Hebei Province. On June 20, a document on educational policy was drawn up for the military sanitary schools. On June 30, Bethune returned to the health department of Shanxi-Chahar-Hebei military region.

July 1939

On July 1, he mailed his "Four-Month Work Report of the Canadian-American Mobile

纪念白求恩

Medical Team" to Nie, Tim Buck (1891-1973, General Secretary of the Canadian Communist Party), Earl Russell Browder (1891-1973, U.S. Communist Party leader for almost 25 years) and Dr. Robert K.S. Lim (林可胜 1897-1969, legendary figure in modern Chinese physiology and medical fields who founded and directed the Chinese Red Cross Medical Relief Corps at that time) from Shenbei Village of Wanxian County. After a dozen days, he completed the "Improvement Proposal on Health Departments' Work" of more than 6,000 words in Shenbei Village, Wanxian County. Due to leg infection at that time, Bethune was transferred to the military region headquarters at Hejiazhuang, Tangxian County for recuperation, during which period he wrote the book *Organization and Technology of Field Hospitals of the Division in Guerrilla Warfare.*

August 1, 1939

Bethune wrote the "Monthly Report of the Canadian-American Mobile Medical Team" at Hejiazhuang Village. After that, he finished such books and handouts as *Preliminary Treatment* and *Model Hospital Standards* for surgeons.

September 1939

At the start of this month, the freshly recovered Bethune went back to the health department at Huapen Village, where he attended the sanitary service directors' meetings of the military region and put forward many specific suggestions to the health department of the military region. On September 18, he delivered a speech at the opening ceremony of the sanitary school of the military region in Niuyangou Village of Tangxian County. At the same time, he suggested the possibility

纪念白求恩

of an inspection event on the part of the health department of the military region, for the sake of inspecting and assisting health work of the troops in each military subarea. On September 25, the inspection team—hosted by the health department of the military region, led by health minister Ye Qingshan and comprised of Bethune, Lin Jinliang（林金亮 1911-1983, rear-line hospital director）and many others—started their survey from the health department of the military region at Huapen Village. Along the planned route, they went for inspection sites of Yujiazhai of Tangxian County, Nanjiazhuanger, Langjiazhuang, Lingshan, Dangcheng and Shanghe of Quyang County, Laogu Village and Gegong Village of Tangxian County, Shennan Village and Beiqingxing Village of Wanxian County, Kanxia, Dule, Songshan and Guantou of Yixian County.

October 20, 1939

The Japanese army launched a "winter sweep" campaign against Shanxi, Chahar and Hebei at that time, when Bethune was about to leave for North America to raise funds for the establishment of the Eighth Route Army rear hospital and the sanitary school of Shanxi-Chahar-Hebei military region as scheduled. He chose to stay on in order to participate in the medical treatment of the "anti-mopping up" operations.

October 29, 1939

During the Motianling battle of Laiyuan County, Bethune operated on a soldier with a wounded leg. In order to speedily wind up it against the approaching Japanese army, Bethune got his middle finger incised while putting his left hand into the wound to take out the damned bone fracture.

245

纪念白求恩

November 1, 1939

While operating on a patient with erysipelas and cellulitis in the neck, Bethune got his left finger infected again via that unhealed open wound.

November 8-10, 1939

When he arrived at the sanitary team of the 3rd Regiment at Wangjiatai of Yixian County on November 8, Bethune ran a high fever of 39.6 ℃. When the fever reached 40 ℃ next day, he was extremely cold, shivering and vomiting, but he carried along with his job still. As his illness was being aggravated the day after, the 3rd Regiment head decided to send him to the rear hospital of the military region for medical treatment. While being sent on a stretcher to the surgical hospital of the military region stationed in Huapen Village of Tangxian County, he decided midway to stop over at the village as they passed Huangshikou of Tangxian County at 3:00 pm on the way. The escorts placed him in a small north hut of villager Di Junxing's courtyard.

November 12, 1939

At 5:20 am, he died of scepticaemia[4] , in villager Di Junxing's hut at Huangshikou Village, Tangxian County of Hebei Province. A letter (*i. e.* last will and testament) written to Nie the day before his death runs as follows:

DEAR COMMANDER NIE:

I am feeling very bad today. Maybe I shall be parted from you forever soon! Will you please write to Tim Buck (General Secretary of the Canadian Communist Party), whose address is 10

4.sepsis, aka systemic inflammatory response syndrome (SIRS)—
Translators'note

纪念白求恩

Wellington Street, Toronto, Canada? And also copy the letter content for the international China Aid Council and the Canadian Democratic Peace Alliance. Tell them that heretofore I have been very happy. My only hope has been making more contribution.

Also please write to Earl Russell Browder, General Secretary of the American Communist Party, along with a sword captured from the battle. You may mail my letters in Chinese renditions. Then they are to be retranslated from the Chinese into English over there. All my photos, diaries and documents will be mailed back there, for store and at the dispersal of Tim Buck. Make sure all these belongings to be packed and mailed within a single box, with the postage covered by the 18 U. S. dollars kindly given to me by Mr. Michael Lindsay[5] . The box must be strong, strapped

---

5.Michael Lindsay (林迈可 1909-1994, British economist), who happened to take the same liner with Bethune from Canada to China in order to teach at Peking University—Translator's note

with a leather belt, and locked with three ropes. Give my everlasting friendship and love to Tim Buck as well as all of my friends in Canada and America.

I'm to ask a favor of the China Aid Council, to allocate some money to my divorced wife for her livelihood—perhaps by instalments. My obligations to her is undeniably heavy, and I should never dump her off simply because I myself have no money. Tell her that I'm guilty-ridden and have once been happy.

Among my personal items, the two camp cots and also two pairs of British leather shoes are for you and Mrs. Nie[6] . As to my riding boots and breeches, I would like to give Commander Lv. Division Commander He should also get his share by selecting whatever he pleases as a

---

6.A list of Chinese individual gift-receivers included at least Nie Rongzhen(聂荣臻）, Mrs. Nie (Zhang Ruihua 张瑞华）, Lv Zhengcao（吕正操）, He Long（贺龙）, Ye Qingshan（叶青山）, You Shenghua（游胜华）, Du Huaizhong（杜怀忠）, Jiang Yizhen（江一真）, Lang Lin（郎林）, Pan Fan（潘凡）, Dong Yueqian（董越千）, Shao Yiping（邵一平）, Old Zhang（老张）, Sha Fei（沙飞）and et al. While in another version, there were supposed to be Lin Jinliang（林金亮）as well, He Zixin（何自新）instead of Shao, and Feng Zhihua（冯志华）instead of Old Zhang.—Translator's note

纪念白求恩

memento.

My two cases should be given to health minister Ye; of my surgical instruments, vice-director You is to have eighteen.

For Dr. Du, another fifteen. Jiang, Medical School principal, may choose two as souvenir.

My typewriter and bandages should go to Comrade Lang. My wristwatch and mosquito net should go to Comrade Pan.

A box of food and literary magazines should go to comrade Dong, as a token of New Year's seasonal greetings.

I would like to give each blanket to my Little Devil[7] and my cook. A pair of Japanese-made leather shoes should also go to Shao. My camera is to be given to Sha Fei.

The water tank and other items should go to

7.a term of endearment for youngsters, esp. junior army men, just like "Little Eighth Route (Armyman)" —Translator's note

the photography squad. Medical books and the little alarm clock are to be given to the sanitary school.

Each year, we need to get ready 250 pounds of quinine and 300 pounds of iron supplement for the sake of malaria and anemia patients. Never buy medicines in such cities as Baoding and Tianjin again, where the drug prices offered were much higher than those of Shanghai and Hongkong, by twofold.

The last two years in China have been the happiest and most significant period of my lifetime. For the present I have a lot to say to the comrades, yet I'm afraid to be too invalid to write more. With thousands of thanks to you and tens of thousands of comrades,

BETH(UNE)

纪念白求恩

November 23, 1939

In the telegram sent by the CPC Central Committee to Bethune's family and relatives via the Central Committee of the Canadian Communist Party, it was stated that: "It is a great bereavement for us, that Dr. Bethune suddenly died of poisoning in Shanxi-Chahar-Hebei border area on November 12 this year, due to careless operation."

In a telegram sent from Commander-in-Chief Zhu De and Deputy Commander-in-Chief Peng Dehuai (彭德怀 1898-1974) to the family and relatives of Bethune via the China Aid Council, it was also stated that what a tremendous loss was Dr. Bethune's "passing away in the Shanxi-Chahar-Hebei border region on November 12 this year. All our fighting men and leaders are deeply saddened to hear the bad news!"

December 1, 1939

A mighty memorial in honor of Dr. Bethune was held in Yan'an. Its organizing committee sent a telegram to his family and relatives via the China Aid Council, saying that Dr. Bethune "unfortunately died of poisoning due to an operation in Shanxi-Chahar-Hebei border area on November 12 this year. When the bad news came, people from all walks of life— no matter in the Party, the government or schools, military guys and local civilians— all took it as a great loss both for the Chinese nation and the people in the whole world and expressed their deep sorrow over it. In addition to holding a memorial in praise of his merits and accomplishments, this special letter is supposed to be a token of sincere consolation and condolence. "

纪念白求恩

December 21, 1939

In an article entitled "Learning from Bethune" [8] for the *Commemorative Compendium in Honor of Norman Bethune* to be published by the political department and the health department of the Eighth Route Army in 1940, Mao Tse-tung wrote to the effect that:

Comrade Norman Bethune... travelled thousands of miles to China. (he made light of travelling thousands of miles to help us in our War of Resistance Against Japan)... What kind of spirit is this that makes a foreigner selflessly adopt the cause of the Chinese people's liberation as his own? It is the spirit of internationalism, the spirit of communism, from which every Chinese Communist

---

8.This article's original title was "Learning from Bethune", which changed into the more popular "In Memory of Bethune" later on when it was to be compiled into *Selected Works of Mao Tse-tung* (Volume 2) after the founding of the People's Republic of China in 1949.— Translator's Note

must learn... Comrade Bethune's spirit, his utter devotion to others without any thought of self, was shown in his boundless sense of responsibility in his work and his boundless warm-heartedness towards all comrades and the people... No one who returned from the front failed to express admiration for Bethune whenever his name was mentioned. And none remained unmoved by his spirit. In the Shanxi-Chahar-Hopei border area, no soldier or civilian was unmoved who had been treated by Dr. Bethune or had seen how he worked... We must all learn the spirit of absolute selflessness from him. With this spirit everyone can be very useful to the people. A man's ability may be great or small, but if he has this spirit, he is already noble-minded and pure, a man of moral integrity and above vulgar interests, a man who is of value to the people. [9]

9.This is an abridgement. For full text further see: Mao Tse-tung, *Serve the People • In Memory of Norman Bethune • The Foolish Old Man Who Removed the Mountains,* Beijing: Foreign Language Press,1978, pp 4-7.—Translator's note

"梦在路上，上道就好"

——讲好白求恩的中国故事

"大道无垠，行者无疆"。伟大的，不远万里来自加拿大的国际战士白求恩（1890—1939）他把脚印深深地留在了中国人民的心里，譬如说聂荣臻司令员惺惺相惜地称他"伯琴"，乡亲百姓们亲切地叫他"白大夫"，在汉语中赋予了整个贝休恩家族一种特殊的、亲切的涵义。他在神州大地上定格成巍巍太行的一页水山，给人类和未来的世界以尊严、正义和光明。"一个高尚的人……一个有益于人民的人"（毛泽东），多么令人爱敬。

旅行本不必背负着价值意义，但是行者主体以"路为纸、地成册、行作笔"，在行旅的过程中无一不体现了价值和意义。"林子里有两条路，我——/选择了行人稀少的那一条/它改变了我的一生"（罗伯特·弗罗斯特），正是白求恩从西班牙内战的纵队返回北美大陆后依然选择来华援华的真实写照。在汹涌澎湃的抗日战争激流中，白求

纪念白求恩

恩短暂的一瞬就这样成为永恒，尤其是在自幼在革命圣地延安的诗人忽培元心底。怀着感恩的心情，带着朝圣的情愫，他终于踏上了溯源之旅：为了圆梦，他奔赴格雷文赫斯特，拜谒白求恩在加拿大的故乡小镇格雷文赫斯特，同时又以澎湃的文思梦回中国历史现场，关联白求恩人生中的关键节点，走近、还原白求恩这位"熟悉的陌生人"的生命路径。激情之余，他知行合一，写下了组诗《纪念白求恩：格雷文赫斯特抒怀》，传递中国人民一如既往"讲好白求恩与中国交集部分的故事"的美好意愿。其在近年来用心感受、探访和考察世界不同的文化和文明的行感录当中脱颖而出，个人的衷肠、人类的共情、造化的暗示都在诗歌中同时展开。同时这也就是本书双语出版的缘起。

所谓"诗言志"，是古代四书五经中有着"中华文明第一典"之称的《尚书·尧典》中所记舜的话，同时也是中国自古以来文论家对诗的奥义与本质特征的第一共识。犹如身体里有一颗种子，必定能在正确的时机产生恰当的回应，有文化情怀的知识分子是不会把自己与对国家、民族和社会的使命分离开来的。这部组诗是"大地和心灵的奉献"，本性上"（诗歌）是一时的、庄严的举动，孤独与声援，情感与行为"（聂鲁达），给人以初见如久别、久别亦如初见的印象，思想丰富，意蕴丰瞻，温柔敦厚的人文情怀和深刻含蓄的历史深思满溢。无论是行动轨迹的客观呈现还是遐想空间的纵横捭阖，都透露出一种强劲的创作自信。

记得汉学家白英曾说，"要理解一个民族，诗是最佳途径。自古以来，中国人就写诗，他们一向把诗视为最美的文化之花"。今日的诗歌创作与翻译的实践者，与曾经的援华战士一样，都可以是国际主义精神的实践者。诗性、语境关联性和诗意对话性，如此种种，共同构成了诗歌的美学价值所在。正如诗眼 asymptote（无限渐近线）所示，笔者在尽力"吃透"文本、"以诗译诗"，从形式特征、情感节奏、语义结构、音调韵律等层面传递中文作品的文学魅力、内在张力与诗学价值性的过程中体会尤甚。新冠疫情引发了世界局势的剧变，旅行变得困难。基于虔心学习与阅读理解的翻译工作，让这两年笔者"身心的描红"获得了一份别样的"卧游"与"朝圣"的欢欣。

　　这部汉英对照版《纪念白求恩：格雷文赫斯特抒怀》的顺利面世，同时也离不开中加两国学界和出版界的通力合作。衷心感谢本书英文审定者新华社中国特稿社副社长、高级编辑熊蕾女士，及其所属的中国白求恩精神研究会的袁永林、栗龙池、马国庆等将学习白求恩"上升为一种公民自觉"的会长尊者，他们的精神鼓励与切实帮助亲切难忘；同时也要感谢"目光如炬"、"不忘初心，上下同欲"的加拿大滑铁卢大学孔子学院外方院长李彦教授，以及出版统筹李娜女士，华艺出版社的副社长严炬先生、执行编辑殷芳先生和北京燕山出版社的责任编辑满懿先生等为此书出版所做的努力，使得作品的生命与价值超越语言、民族和时空的障碍而得以更广阔地拓展和更恒久地流传。

　　七十多年前，新中国的缔造者之一、国家名誉主席宋庆龄先生在《我们时代的英雄》一文中深情地写道："任何时代的英雄都是这样一种人：他们以惊人的忠诚、决心、勇气和技能完成了那个时代放在人人面前的重要任务……诺尔曼·白求恩就是这样一位英雄。他曾在三个国家里生活、工作和斗争……在一种特殊的意义上，他属于这三个国家的人民。"

　　阅读，是一场以幻为真的寻找；沿着他人的轨迹，是渴望与另一些人、一些灵魂的相遇。衷心希冀它能伴随读者记住白求恩，这位穿越时空而在世界友谊地久天长的丹青上写下厚重一笔的、富有传奇色彩的历史人物，距离通过多声部、有质感的和谐吟唱拼贴出与塑就一幅完美的人物拼图更近一点儿。——"念念不忘，必有回响"，山川从来如是，人类命运共同体亦如是！

任小玫

2022 年 2 月 22 日于北京

纪念白求恩.

Dream Is on the Road If a Mind Is Set—
To Hit the Right Note for a Good Story of Dr. Bethune in China

"Ways are infinite, and there'd be no borders for pedestrians". Lo and behold! What an international soldier Norman Bethune (1890–1939) was! He journeyed from Canada to China as faith fears no distance, and inscribed an indelible impression on the people's hearts. Commander Nie Rongzhen appreciated him and called him endearingly "Boqin"[1], while local villagers tenderly addressed him "Doctor Bai" (sounding similar to Beth /beθ/) in a familiar compatriot manner. And it certainly empowers the surname "Bethune" to take on a special and warm meaning in China. After he laid down his life, he was buried in Taihang Mountain Range and his soul became a stalwart stature as that a leaflet

1. Somehow suggestive of Boya (a famous guqin music master) and Ziqi, his bosom friend, as illustrated in the Chinese set phrase "High mountain and running water" which refers to understanding and appreciative friends as well as melodious music.—Translator's note

of rill and hill across the landscape of the nation—bringing dignity, justice and light to mankind and the future world. Chairman Mao Tse-tung credited Bethune for being "noble-minded and pure... a man who is of value to the people" —how adorable he is!

Travel is going to be set off with a backpack only. Yet more often than not, as suggested by the American popular novel *On the Road* by Jack Kerouac, it is not the case for true travelers who "take the paths on the land as papers of a travelogue", speak loud of his trekking via action (a footprint-like brush), which embodies the value and significance of travel. Robert Frost's famous stanza "Two roads diverged in a wood, and I-/I took the one less traveled by,/And that has made all the difference" is in concert with what Bethune chose to do after he returned to the American continent from the Spanish Civil War as a member of International Brigade: coming over to China in need. Amid

纪念白求恩

the surging torrents of the Chinese People's
War of Resistance Against Japanese Aggression,
Bethune's brief, final moment in the last flung
of his life-stage is an everlasting monument.
This sense was so intense in Mr. Hu Peiyuan,
a poet who was born and bred in Yan'an, the
cradle of Red Revolution in China, and revered
Bethune ever since he was a robust fledgling.
To square his dream with reality, he embarked
on the journey with a thankful heart. He went
on a pilgrimage to pay a tribute visit to
Gravenhurst, the "familiar yet somehow alien"
Bethune's hometown in Canada. At the locus, he
was absent-minded, occasionally going back to
memorable instants of the Chinese scenarios,
then recovering his composure to get a close-
up, in trace of Bethune's life path from the
small circumference of his Ontario boyhood to
a heroic role in the great Anti-fascist War in
world history. It also explains why with buoyant
enthusiasm he committed to words, got down
to this suite of poems in Chinese, as poetic

inspirations kept welling up exponentially from the contemplative mind armed with well-knit historical knowledge. Blessed with the legacy of the Chinese people's goodwill to "tell Bethune's story in China", it draws wide acclaim since it is notably outstanding so far as highly personalized poetic technique is concerned: Simultaneous unfolding of the nearness to oneself, the nearness to mankind and to the secret manifestations of nature makes it through the galore of literary records on pacy tours of different civilizations around the globe. Henceforth a translation proposal for a bilingual book.

The often-quoted indoctrination that "Poetry should be engaged to convey the ideal of people" is what Emperor Shun, a legendary monarch in ancient China, says in the "Chronology of Emperor Yao" among the *Book of Documents* (one of the Ancient Four Books and Five Classics in China), which is also well-known as "the

纪念白求恩

first chronology of Chinese civilization".
Meanwhile, it is the earliest consensus reached
among Chinese literary theorists on the profound
meaning and essential characters of poetry since
ancient times. Just as a seed in the earth is
destined to burgeon in time, an intellectual
with a lofty ideal and cultural attachment
cherished within will not get himself off orbit
from their mission to the country, nation and
society in a cultural event. This volume of
verse is "contributions from the earth and from
the soul", and "is an action, ephemeral or
solemn, in which there enter as equal partners
solitude and solidarity, emotion and action"
(Pablo Neruda) essentially. It gives readers an
impression that when they first meet, it feels
like decades at the same time. Deep in thought,
rich in literary implication, it is brimful of
gentle, sincere and humanistic feelings as well
as profound, subtle historical implications.
Both objective presentation of life track and
maneuvering of reveries in space bespeak a

certain creative confidence and upbeat mood of the poet.

As British sinologist Robert Payne mentioned, "We can understand a people best through their poetry, and the Chinese, who have written poetry since the beginning of time, have always regarded poetry as the finest flower of their culture. " Nowadays the spirit of internationalism can be boosted by poets and translators, like former soldiers who helped China in the WWII, since poetry, the most legitimate "travel passport", is the Esperanto for their barrier-free communication. Poetics, contextual relevance, sentimental dialogism and other elements, all rolled into one, embodies the aesthetic value of poetry. The rendition is my attempt to gain an insight into and "translate poesie into poesie"[2], in the end to present in

---

2. Abiding by the tenet of "translating poesie into poesie", the translator manages to (1)provide a hi-fi analogy of the originals in both form and content, that is, to be precise with every word and keep delicate in texture, satisfying all elements of textuality, by the principles of proximity and proxy deftly applied; (2)be as literal as is possible and as free as is necessary, for the best possible equivalence in semantic content, stylistic appropriateness and illocutionary force; (3)in addition to proper diction and scansion, best represent the form-meaning tension and retain the potency hidden within as well as an artful reconstruction of the literariness.—Translator's note

纪念白求恩

the lucid English poetic way—in the name of
"asymptote"　—the literary charm, emotional
charge and aesthetic effects of the Chinese
work in terms of lyricism, syntax, semantics,
emotion, rhyme, rhythm and cadence, etc.
COVID-19 has triggered a drastic change in the
world and made travel difficult for any one. As
I riveted on reading and translating this piece
in the last years, what a vivid and vicarious
pilgrimage experience I have gained and how afar
I have been carried away in labor of love!

The publication of this Chinese-English edition
of *In Memory of Dr. Norman Bethune: A Pilgrim
Tribute to Gravenhurst of Canada (Expressivo)*
also involves cooperation efforts of the academic
and publishing circles of China and Canada. I
owe specific, personal thanks to the insightful
reviser Madame Xiong Lei (former executive
editor and senior journalist of *China Features*,
Xinhua News Agency) for her reviewing of the
English part, and the many venerable scholars—

Yuan Yonglin, Li Longchi and Ma Guoqing (the three, all honorary presidents)—of the Chinese Bethune Spirit Research Association, in terms of spiritual encouragement and solid help as well as their persistence in "Learning from Dr. Bethune on one's own initiative". At the same time, I would also like to thank the far-sighted professor Li Yan (the Canadian director of Confucius Institute at the University of Waterloo), Li Na (publishing co-ordinator), Yan Ju and Yin Fang (respectively vice-president, senior editor of Huayi Publishing House), Man Yi (senior editor of Beijing Yanshan Publishing House) who "remain true to original aspiration and work in unison", which helps the work to fight against the illusion of separateness and reach out beyond language, nation and space to more people, to be circulated in more accessible, lasting ways.

Over three score and ten years ago, Soong Ching-ling (Madame Sun Yat-sen, one of the founders

纪念白求恩

of the new China and honorary president of the
state) wrote affectionately in "The Hero in Our
Age" that:

"The hero in any age is one who carries
out with a surpassing degree of devotion,
determination, courage, and skill the main
tasks with which his times challenge every
man...Norman Bethune was such a hero. He lived,
worked and fought in three countries...In a
special sense he belongs to the peoples of these
three countries[3].

Along the trajectory of others' life journey,
we read fantasies that ended up being real, in
search for an encounter with them, soul mates-
to-be. It is sincerely hoped that readers
will get themselves to know well Bethune in
person, the legendary historical figure who
shines out in world history with his preferred

---

3. Soong Ching-ling, 1952. Preface of The Scalpel, the Sword: The Story
of Dr. Norman Bethune (by Ted Allen and Sidney Gordon). Canada:
McClelland and Stewart Limited, pix.—Translator's note

marching forth over distance and forging lasting friendship under the firmament. It is also believed that our common endeavor, like a combination of simultaneous musical notes, will make a melodious performance, or in other words, if pieced together will make a full picture in vision or a perfect puzzle-set about Bethune. — Separated by mountains, rivers on land we may have been, yet the earth has music for those who listen, as "one need only believe in something that you keep in mind, and the mountains would echo in the end", since it is under the same sky that we stand, so is the case for the human community with a shared future!

Ren Xiaomei

Written in Beijing,

February 22, 2022